SERIES

(ex•ploring)

1. Investigating in a systematic way: examining. 2. Searching into or ranging over for the purpose of discovery.

Getting Started with

Discipline Specific Projects

Using Microsoft Office 2013

Mary Anne Poatsy

Gionfriddo / Joos / Lau / Porter

Series Created by Dr. Robert T. Grauer

PEARSON

Boston Columbus Indianapolis New York San Francisco Upper Saddle River
Amsterdam Cape Town Dubai London Madrid Milan Munich Paris Montréal Toronto
Delhi Mexico City São Paulo Sydney Hong Kong Seoul Singapore Taipei Tokyo

Senior Editor: Samantha McAfee Lewis
Team Lead, Project Management: Laura Burgess
Project Manager: Laura Karahalis
Program Manager: Natacha Moore
Development Editor: Barbara Stover
Editorial Assistant: Victoria Lasavath
Director of Product Marketing: Maggie Waples
Director of Field Marketing: Leigh Ann Sims
Field Marketing Managers: Brad Forrester & Joanna Sabella
Marketing Coordinator: Susan Osterlitz

Senior Operations Specialist: Maura Zaldivar
Senior Art Director: Diane Ernsberger
Interior and Cover Design: Diane Ernsberger
Cover Photo: Courtesy of Shutterstock® Images
Associate Director of Design: Blair Brown
Digital Media Editor: Eric Hakanson
Director of Media Development: Taylor Ragan
Media Project Manager, Production: John Cassar
Full-Service Project Management: Jenna Gray, PreMediaGlobal
Composition: PreMediaGlobal

Credits and acknowledgments borrowed from other sources and reproduced, with permission, in this textbook appear below.

Library of Congress Cataloging-in-Publication Data

Poatsy, Mary Anne.
  Getting started with discipline-specific projects using Microsoft Office 2013 / Mary Anne Poatsy.
    pages cm. — (Series exploring)
  Includes bibliographical references and index.
  ISBN 978-0-13-342642-7 — ISBN 0-13-342642-4
  1. Microsoft Office. 2. Universities and colleges—Curricula—Computer programs. I. Title.
  HF5548.4.M525P63 2015
  005.5—dc23

                                        2014001206

10 9 8 7 6 5 4 3 2 1

ISBN-10:   0-13-342642-4
ISBN-13: 978-0-13-342642-7

Dedications

To my husband, Paul, and my children, Michael, Diana, and Robert, who have tried to be patient and understanding while I worked away on these projects. Thank you for your love, support and encouragement.

Sheila Gionfriddo

I dedicate this book to my husband and son, without whose support and encouragement all of this would not be possible and to my students who continue to inspire me to produce more and better learning experiences.

Dr. Irene Joos

I dedicate this book to my only child, Catherine Shen, who taught me that there is another wonderful life outside of my work. My life has been more fulfilling and exciting with her in it. I also dedicate this book to the loving memory of my dog, Harry, who was by my side, through thick and thin, for 16 years. I miss him dearly, every day.

Linda K. Lau

I dedicate this book to my husband, Herman, for his loving support he has continued to share with me for now more than 40 years. This project of editing was new and very time consuming but his support was never wavering. So, I thank him.

Orbra Harrington Porter

For my husband Ted, who unselfishly continues to take on more than his share to support me throughout the process; and for my children, Laura, Carolyn, and Teddy, whose encouragement and love have been inspiring.

Mary Anne Poatsy

About the Authors

Sheila Gionfriddo, Science Discipline

Sheila is currently a faculty member in the Computer Information Systems Department at Luzerne County Community College in Nanticoke, Pennsylvania. She has been an educator for over 12 years at the college, is the coordinator for the Office Information Management program and the Administrator for MyITLab at the school. Sheila currently teaches various computer applications and office information courses in face-to-face and online environments. She is Microsoft certified in all Office Applications.

Sheila holds a B.S. in Pre-Veterinary Medicine from the University of Connecticut and an A.A.S. degree in Computer Information Systems from Luzerne County Community College. After working almost 20 years as a Laboratory Supervisor and Certified Histocompatibility Technologist, she switched careers. With a strong science background and a love of learning technology, she earned another degree and begin teaching. She enjoys learning, and is currently working towards another degree, in Health Information Technology. One of her greatest joys is helping students of all ages learn how to use computer applications to be successful in their chosen field of study.

Dr. Irene Joos, Education Discipline

Dr. Irene Joos is an Associate Professor in the Information Systems and Technology Department and former Director of Online Learning at La Roche College where she currently teaches practical computing applications, system analysis and design, introduction to cyberspace, computer-based/distance education training, virtual communities and social media, senior seminar, introduction to nursing informatics, and a graduate course nursing informatics for nurse administrators and educators. As the former Director of Online Learning she was responsible for faculty support and training, student support and training, and served as the Blackboard administrator. Prior to coming to La Roche College, she taught at the University of Pittsburgh and served as the Director of the LRC where she was responsible for all the computers and related teaching labs.

Irene received her BSN in Nursing from Pennsylvania State University and her MN in Nursing, MSIS in Information Science, and Ph.D. in Education with a focus on curriculum and supervision and educational gaming/simulation.

Irene has authored many articles and several textbooks the latest two being *Introduction to Computers for Healthcare Professionals* and *Social Media for Nurses*. She has contributed to edited books on the topics of Data Processing and Distance Education. She has presented in the United States and several other countries on topics such as Social Media in Healthcare, Education and Curriculum Implications of Health 2.0, and has conducted several workshops on Getting Started with Teaching Online and Using Blackboard.

Dr. Linda K. Lau, Business Discipline

Dr. Linda K. Lau joined the faculty of the College of Business and Economics at Longwood University, located in Farmville, Virginia, in 1994. She is currently an Associate Professor of Information Systems and Security (ISYS) with the College. Over the years, Linda had taught many MIS and Management courses, which includes Principles of MIS, Database Management, Systems Analysis and Design, Visual Basic, Introduction to Computer Security, Forensics, and Law, Business Ethics, and Business Statistics. She was honored with the *Outstanding Academic Advisor Award* in 2006. Besides teaching and advising, Linda has authored and co-authored several journal and conference articles, edited two books, and sits on numerous editorial boards. She also serves as the copy editor of the *Journal of Digital Forensics, Security and Law*, which publishes four issues a year. Her current research interest focuses on digital forensics, enterprise resource planning, campus ethics, hybrid/online learning, and e-commerce. She recently completed a computer forensics course on the *X-Ways Integrated Computer Forensics* software.

Linda earned her Ph.D. from Rensselaer Polytechnic Institute in 1993, and her M.B.A. and Bachelor of Science from Illinois State University in 1987 and 1986, respectively. In her younger days, Linda worked as a flight attendant for Singapore International Airlines for six years before coming to America to pursue her academic dream. She also worked as a financial consultant with Salomon Smith Barney from 1999–2000 before returning to the academic world.

Linda resides in Farmville and Richmond with her family.

Orbra Harrington Porter, Arts and Legal Disciplines

Orbra, an adjunct faculty member at the Jackson Campus of Hinds Community College applies real-life business application from experiences at a manufacturing facility where she assisted in birthing the use of computers daily with the management staff level to hourly employees, in the plant. In 2001, she retired from full-time employment after 27 years but continues to nurture her love for teaching by tutoring at the evening classes, which she had started earlier. During her more than 20 years of tenure in the college's Business and Office Technology Department, she taught various computer applications and concepts courses. She holds a B.S. in Mathematics from Tougaloo College and a M.S. in Technology Education from Jackson State University. Orbra resides in Mississippi with her husband Herman, who shares her love for technology.

Mary Anne Poatsy, Series Editor

Mary Anne is a senior faculty member at Montgomery County Community College, teaching various computer applications and concepts courses in face-to-face and online environments. She holds a B.A. in psychology and education from Mount Holyoke College and an M.B.A. in finance from Northwestern University's Kellogg Graduate School of Management.

Mary Anne has more than 12 years of educational experience. She is currently adjunct faculty at Gwynedd-Mercy College and Montgomery County Community College. She has also taught at Bucks County Community College and Muhlenberg College, as well as conducted personal training. Before teaching, she was Vice President at Shearson Lehman in the Municipal Bond Investment Banking Department.

Dr. Robert T. Grauer, Creator of the Exploring Series

Bob Grauer is an Associate Professor in the Department of Computer Information Systems at the University of Miami, where he is a multiple winner of the Outstanding Teaching Award in the School of Business, most recently in 2009. He has written numerous COBOL texts and is the vision behind the Exploring Office series, with more than three million books in print. His work has been translated into three foreign languages and is used in all aspects of higher education at both national and international levels. Bob Grauer has consulted for several major corporations including IBM and American Express. He received his Ph.D. in Operations Research in 1972 from the Polytechnic Institute of Brooklyn.

Contents

Acknowledgments

The Exploring team would like to acknowledge and thank all the reviewers who helped us throughout the years by providing us with their invaluable comments, suggestions, and constructive criticism.

We'd like to especially thank our Focus Group attendees and User Diary Reviewers for this edition:

Stephen Z. Jourdan
Auburn University at Montgomery

Ann Rovetto
Horry-Georgetown Technical
College

Jacqueline D. Lawson
Henry Ford Community College

Diane L. Smith
Henry Ford Community College

Sven Aelterman
Troy University

Suzanne M. Jeska
County College of Morris

Susan N. Dozier
Tidewater Community College

Robert G. Phipps Jr.
West Virginia University

Mike Michaelson
Palomar College

Mary Beth Tarver
Northwestern State University

Alexandre C. Probst
Colorado Christian University

Phil Nielson
Salt Lake Community College

Carolyn Barren
Macomb Community College

Sue A. McCrory
Missouri State University

Lucy Parakhovnik
California State University, Northridge

Jakie Brown Jr.
Stevenson University

Craig J. Peterson
American InterContinental University

Terry Ray Rigsby
Hill College

Biswadip Ghosh
Metropolitan State University of Denver

Cheryl Sypniewski
Macomb Community College

Lynn Keane
University of South Carolina

Sheila Gionfriddo
Luzerne College

Dick Hewer
Ferris State College

Carolyn Borne
Louisiana State University

Sumathy Chandrashekar
Salisbury University

Laura Marcoulides
Fullerton College

Don Riggs
SUNY Schenectady County Community
College

Gary McFall
Purdue University

James Powers
University of Southern Indiana

James Brown
Central Washington University

Brian Powell
West Virginia University

Sherry Lenhart
Terra Community College

Chen Zhang
Bryant University

Nikia Robinson
Indian River State University

Jill Young
Southeast Missouri State University

Debra Hoffman
Southeast Missouri State University

Tommy Lu
Delaware Technical Community College

Mimi Spain
Southern Maine Community College

We'd like to thank everyone who has been involved in reviewing and providing their feedback, including for our previous editions:

Adriana Lumpkin
Midland College

Alan S. Abrahams
Virginia Tech

Ali Berrached
University of Houston–Downtown

Allen Alexander
Delaware Technical & Community College

Andrea Marchese
Maritime College, State University of New York

Andrew Blitz
Broward College; Edison State College

Angel Norman
University of Tennessee, Knoxville

Angela Clark
University of South Alabama

Ann Rovetto
Horry-Georgetown Technical College

Astrid Todd
Guilford Technical Community College

Audrey Gillant
Maritime College, State University of New York

Barbara Stover
Marion Technical College

Barbara Tollinger
Sinclair Community College

Ben Brahim Taha
Auburn University

Beverly Amer
Northern Arizona University

Beverly Fite
Amarillo College

Bonita Volker
Tidewater Community College

Bonnie Homan
San Francisco State University

Brad West
Sinclair Community College

Brian Powell
West Virginia University

Carol Buser
Owens Community College

Carol Roberts
University of Maine

Carolyn Barren
Macomb Community College

Cathy Poyner
Truman State University

Charles Hodgson
Delgado Community College

Cheri Higgins
Illinois State University

Cheryl Hinds
Norfolk State University

Chris Robinson
Northwest State Community College

Cindy Herbert
Metropolitan Community College–Longview

Dana Hooper
University of Alabama

Dana Johnson
North Dakota State University

Daniela Marghitu
Auburn University

David Noel
University of Central Oklahoma

David Pulis
Maritime College, State University of New York

David Thornton
Jacksonville State University

Dawn Medlin
Appalachian State University

Debby Keen
University of Kentucky

Debra Chapman
University of South Alabama

Derrick Huang
Florida Atlantic University

Diana Baran
Henry Ford Community College

Diane Cassidy
The University of North Carolina at Charlotte

Diane Smith
Henry Ford Community College

Don Danner
San Francisco State University

Don Hoggan
Solano College

Doncho Petkov
Eastern Connecticut State University

Donna Ehrhart
State University of New York at Brockport

Elaine Crable
Xavier University

Elizabeth Duett
Delgado Community College

Erhan Uskup
Houston Community College–Northwest

Eric Martin
University of Tennessee

Erika Nadas
Wilbur Wright College

Floyd Winters
Manatee Community College

Frank Lucente
Westmoreland County Community College

G. Jan Wilms
Union University

Gail Cope
Sinclair Community College

Gary DeLorenzo
California University of Pennsylvania

Gary Garrison
Belmont University

George Cassidy
Sussex County Community College

Gerald Braun
Xavier University

Gerald Burgess
Western New Mexico University

Gladys Swindler
Fort Hays State University

Heith Hennel
Valencia Community College

Henry Rudzinski
Central Connecticut State University

Irene Joos
La Roche College

Iwona Rusin
Baker College; Davenport University

J. Roberto Guzman
San Diego Mesa College

Jan Wilms
Union University

Jane Stam
Onondaga Community College

Janet Bringhurst
Utah State University

Jeanette Dix
Ivy Tech Community College

Jennifer Day
Sinclair Community College

Jill Canine
Ivy Tech Community College

Jim Chaffee
The University of Iowa Tippie College of Business

Joanne Lazirko
University of Wisconsin–Milwaukee

Jodi Milliner
Kansas State University

John Hollenbeck
Blue Ridge Community College

John Seydel
Arkansas State University

Judith A. Scheeren
Westmoreland County Community College

Judith Brown
The University of Memphis

Juliana Cypert
Tarrant County College

Kamaljeet Sanghera
George Mason University

Karen Priestly
Northern Virginia Community College

Karen Ravan
Spartanburg Community College

Kathleen Brenan
Ashland University

Ken Busbee
Houston Community College

Kent Foster
Winthrop University

Kevin Anderson
Solano Community College

Kim Wright
The University of Alabama

Kristen Hockman
University of Missouri–Columbia

Kristi Smith
Allegany College of Maryland

Laura McManamon
University of Dayton

Leanne Chun
Leeward Community College

Lee McClain
Western Washington University

Linda D. Collins
Mesa Community College

Linda Johnsonius
Murray State University

Linda Lau
Longwood University

Linda Theus
Jackson State Community College

Linda Williams
Marion Technical College

Lisa Miller
University of Central Oklahoma

Lister Horn
Pensacola Junior College

Lixin Tao
Pace University

Loraine Miller
Cayuga Community College

Lori Kielty
Central Florida Community College

Lorna Wells
Salt Lake Community College

Lorraine Sauchin
Duquesne University

Lucy Parakhovnik (Parker)
California State University, Northridge

Lynn Mancini
Delaware Technical Community College

Mackinzee Escamilla
South Plains College

Marcia Welch
Highline Community College

Margaret McManus
Northwest Florida State College

Margaret Warrick
Allan Hancock College

Marilyn Hibbert
Salt Lake Community College

Mark Choman
Luzerne County Community College

Mary Duncan
University of Missouri–St. Louis

Melissa Nemeth
Indiana University-Purdue University Indianapolis

Melody Alexander
Ball State University

Michael Douglas
University of Arkansas at Little Rock

Michael Dunklebarger
Alamance Community College

Michael G. Skaff
College of the Sequoias

Michele Budnovitch
Pennsylvania College of Technology

Mike Jochen
East Stroudsburg University

Mike Scroggins
Missouri State University

Muhammed Badamas
Morgan State University

NaLisa Brown
University of the Ozarks

Nancy Grant
Community College of Allegheny County–South Campus

Nanette Lareau
University of Arkansas Community College–Morrilton

Pam Brune
Chattanooga State Community College

Pam Uhlenkamp
Iowa Central Community College

Patrick Smith
Marshall Community and Technical College

Paul Addison
Ivy Tech Community College

Paula Ruby
Arkansas State University

Peggy Burrus
Red Rocks Community College

Peter Ross
SUNY Albany

Philip H. Nielson
Salt Lake Community College

Ralph Hooper
University of Alabama

Ranette Halverson
Midwestern State University

Richard Blamer
John Carroll University

Richard Cacace
Pensacola Junior College

Richard Hewer
Ferris State University

Rob Murray
Ivy Tech Community College

Robert Dušek
Northern Virginia Community College

Robert Sindt
Johnson County Community College

Robert Warren
Delgado Community College

Rocky Belcher
Sinclair Community College

Roger Pick
University of Missouri at Kansas City

Ronnie Creel
Troy University

Rosalie Westerberg
Clover Park Technical College

Ruth Neal
Navarro College

Sandra Thomas
Troy University

Sheila Gionfriddo
Luzerne County Community College

Sherrie Geitgey
Northwest State Community College

Sophia Wilberscheid
Indian River State College

Sophie Lee
California State University, Long Beach

Stacy Johnson
Iowa Central Community College

Stephanie Kramer
Northwest State Community College

Stephen Jourdan
Auburn University Montgomery

Steven Schwarz
Raritan Valley Community College

Sue McCrory
Missouri State University

Susan Fuschetto
Cerritos College

Susan Medlin
UNC Charlotte

Suzan Spitzberg
Oakton Community College

Sven Aelterman
Troy University

Sylvia Brown
Midland College

Tanya Patrick
Clackamas Community College

Terri Holly
Indian River State College

Thomas Rienzo
Western Michigan University

Tina Johnson
Midwestern State University

Tommy Lu
Delaware Technical and Community College

Troy S. Cash
NorthWest Arkansas Community College

Vicki Robertson
Southwest Tennessee Community

Weifeng Chen
California University of Pennsylvania

Wes Anthony
Houston Community College

William Ayen
University of Colorado at Colorado Springs

Wilma Andrews
Virginia Commonwealth University

Yvonne Galusha
University of Iowa

Special thanks to our development and technical team:

Barbara Stover

Cheryl Slavick

Elizabeth Lockley

Heather Hetzler

Jennifer Lynn

Joyce Nielsen

Linda Pogue

Lisa Bucki

Lori Damanti

Mara Zebest

Susan Fry

Preface

The Exploring Series and You

Exploring is Pearson's Office Application series that requires students like you to think "beyond the point and click." In this edition, we have worked to restructure the Exploring experience around the way you, today's modern student, actually use your resources.

The goal of Exploring is, as it has always been, to go further than teaching just the steps to accomplish a task—the series provides the theoretical foundation for you to understand when and why to apply a skill.

As a result, you achieve a deeper understanding of each application and can apply this critical thinking beyond Office and the classroom.

You are practical students, focused on what you need to do to be successful in this course and beyond, and want to be as efficient as possible. Exploring has evolved to meet you where you are and help you achieve success efficiently. Pearson has paid attention to the habits of students today, how you get information, how you are motivated to do well in class, and what your future goals look like. We asked you and your peers for acceptance of new tools we designed to address these points, and you responded with a resounding "YES!"

Here Is What We Learned About You

You are goal-oriented. You want a good grade in this course—so we rethought how Exploring works so that you can learn the how and why behind the skills in this course to be successful now. You also want to be successful in your future career—so we used motivating case studies to show relevance of these skills to your future careers and incorporated Soft Skills, Collaboration, and Analysis Cases in this edition to set you up for success in the future.

You read, prepare, and study differently than students used to. You use textbooks like a tool—you want to easily identify what you need to know and learn it efficiently. We have added key features such as Step Icons, Hands-On Exercise Videos, and tracked everything via page numbers that allow you to navigate the content efficiently, making the concepts accessible and creating a map to success for you to follow.

You go to college now with a different set of skills than students did five years ago. The new edition of Exploring moves you beyond the basics of the software at a faster pace, without sacrificing coverage of the fundamental skills that you need to know. This ensures that you will be engaged from page 1 to the end of the book.

You and your peers have diverse learning styles. With this in mind, we broadened our definition of "student resources" to include Compass, an online skill database; movable Student Reference cards; Hands-On Exercise videos to provide a secondary lecture-like option of review; Soft Skills video exercises to illustrate important non-technical skills; and the most powerful online homework and assessment tool around with a direct 1:1 content match with the Exploring Series, MyITLab. Exploring will be accessible to all students, regardless of learning style.

Providing You with a Map to Success to Move Beyond the Point and Click

All of these changes and additions will provide you with an easy and efficient path to follow to be successful in this course, regardless of your learning style or any existing knowledge you have at the outset. Our goal is to keep you more engaged in both the hands-on and conceptual sides, helping you to achieve a higher level of understanding that will guarantee you success in this course and in your future career. In addition to the vision and experience of the series creator, Robert T. Grauer, we have assembled a tremendously talented team of Office Applications authors who have devoted themselves to teaching you the ins and outs of Microsoft Word, Excel, Access, and PowerPoint. Led in this edition by series editor Mary Anne Poatsy, the whole team is equally dedicated to providing you with a **map to success** to support the Exploring mission of **moving you beyond the point and click.**

Instructor Resources

The Instructor's Resource Center, available at **www.pearsonhighered.com**, includes the following:

- **Instructor Manual** provides an overview of all available resources as well as student data and solution files for every exercise.

- **Solution Files with Scorecards** assist with grading the Hands-On Exercises and end-of-chapter exercises.

Student Resources

Companion Web Site

www.pearsonhighered.com/exploring offers expanded IT resources and self-student tools for students to use for each chapter, including:

- Web Resources

- Student Data Files

Art Discipline

Using Microsoft Office as a Production Assistant

BACKGROUND | Working as a Production Assistant

Production work in theaters, film making, and television requires the assistance of many workers. The Production Assistant, also called a PA, may have a vast number of responsibilities that can be as rudimentary as going for a cup of coffee to being in an administrative level of managing actors, staff, and then handling many aspects of public relations.

Microsoft Office provides a suite of applications to assist a theater company PA with many of their administrative tasks such as creating a press packet for the company. Such a packet would include a cover page, a cover letter, a press release, and a brochure to advertise upcoming productions. The PA may be responsible for overseeing the finances of a production by maintaining schedules, analyzing the budget for upcoming shows, updating the budget of a current show, and creating forecasting of ticket sales based on past shows. Much of the data can be stored in databases to give the PA immediate access to generating forms and reports that will be used by Producers and Directors. A kiosk is located in the theater and the PA will be responsible for creating and maintain presentation files that can run automatically and advertise season tickets for the year.

Discipline Specific Capstones

Using Office in the Arts Profession

Application	Exercises	Skills Covered
1. WORD Data Files: 01w_PressPacket 01w_gmlogo.jpg 01w_PriceList Solution Files: 01w_PressPacket_LastFirst	PRESS PACKET (page 5)	• Insert page breaks • Insert a cover page • Insert headers and footers • Check spelling and grammar • Set margins and specify page orientation • Apply font attributes • Set off paragraphs with tabs and bulleted lists • Select paragraph spacing • Apply borders • Apply styles • Select a document theme • Insert, resize, move, and align a picture • Insert a text box • Insert and modify a WordArt • Use styles • Insert a table • Insert a row or column • Merge cells • Format a table • Insert formulas in a table • Convert text to a table • Create footnotes • Add a comment • Use Track changes • Accept changes
2. EXCEL Data Files: 01e_Theatre Solution Files: 01e_Theatre_LastFirst	SCHEDULE AND BUDGET (page 9)	• Enter and edit cell data • Enter dates • Use cell references in formulas • Apply the order of precedence • Copy formulas with Auto Fill • Manage worksheets • Manage columns and rows • Apply alignment and font options • Apply number formats • Set page orientation • Create headers and footers • Use relative, absolute, and mixed cell references in formulas • Calculate a total with the SUM function • Insert basic statistical functions • Insert the TODAY function • Determine results with the IF function • Use LOOKUP function • Use the PMT function • Select data source for a chart • Choose a chart type • Create a pie chart • Move a chart • Apply a chart style
3. ACCESS Data Files: 01a_Broadway 01a_ImportCasting.xlsx Solution Files: 01a_Broadway_LastFirst	BROADWAY DATABASE MANAGEMENT (page 13)	• Open an Access file and work with content security • Navigate among the objects in an Access database • Edit a record • Save the database • Back up, compact, and repair an Access file • Sort table data on one or more fields • Use the Relationships window • Understand relational power • Enforce referential integrity • Create tables • Set a table's primary key • Work with field properties • Import an Excel spreadsheet • Establish table relationships • Create a single-table query • Use Query Design view • Specify query criteria for different data types • Run, copy, and modify a query • Create a multi-table query • Modify a multi-table query • Create a calculated field in a query • Create expressions with Expression Builder • Format and save calculated results • Verify calculated results • Use built-in functions in Access • Perform date arithmetic • Add aggregate functions to datasheets and queries • Create a totals query with grouping • Create forms using the Form tool • Modify a form • Revise forms using Layout view • Identify control types in forms • Create reports using the Report Wizard • Preview a report • Modify a report • Revise reports using Layout and Design views • Identify control types in reports

4. POWERPOINT Data Files: 01p_gmlogo.jpg 01p_gmaudio.mp3 01p_Outline.docx 01p_Brochure 01p_Paul's_Kitchen_1.jpg 01p_Paul's_Kitchen_2.jpg 01p_Christmas_at_the_ Andersons'.jpg 01p_This_Was_Not_In_The_ Brochure.jpg Solution Files: 01p_Season_LastFirst	ADVERTISE SEASON TICKETS (page 16)	• Use PowerPoint views • Create a new presentation • Edit the title slide • Add new slides • Use spell check • Reorder slides • Insert a media object • Add a table • Animate objects • Apply transitions • Use slide layouts • Apply themes • Add pictures • Import an outline • Reuse slides from an existing presentation • Use a callout shape • Change a shape outline • Create SmartArt • Modify SmartArt • Create WordArt • Modify WordArt • Modify objects • Group objects • Arrange objects • Insert a picture • Transform a picture • Remove a picture background • Add audio • Change audio settings
5. INTEGRATED Data Files: 01i_ SeasonTickets.accdb Solution Files: 01i_ SeatCount_LastFirst.xlsx 01i_Stats_LastFirst.pptx	SEASON TICKET REPORTING (page 20)	• Create a summary query • Export query results to an Excel worksheet • Calculate statistics using MIN, MAX, and AVERAGE functions • Create charts from data • Display the statistics and charts as linked objects in a PowerPoint presentation • Share the presentation as an e-mail PDF attachment

Use Microsoft Word

Background

A word processing application is the most used program in a theater company business office. Production assistants create correspondence, contracts with actors, and theater rental space contracts as well as memos, reports, press releases, and documents requiring desktop publishing. It is imperative that a production assistant becomes proficient in Microsoft Word and its many features.

Tasks

In a theater company's business office, a production assistant might be asked to create and develop many types of documents, including the following:

- Correspondence and mailings
- Contracts (actors and technicians of local and touring shows, crew, venue contact people)
- Tables
- Press releases
- Brochures

Skills

Production assistants should be able to do the following:

Chapter 1

- Insert page breaks
- Insert a cover page
- Insert headers and footers
- Check spelling and grammar
- Set margins and specify page orientation

Chapter 2

- Apply font attributes
- Set off paragraphs with tabs and bulleted lists
- Select paragraph spacing
- Apply borders
- Apply styles
- Select a document theme
- Insert, resize, move, and align a picture
- Insert a text box
- Insert and modify WordArt
- Use styles

Chapter 3

- Insert a table
- Insert a row or column
- Merge cells
- Format a table
- Insert formulas in a table
- Convert text to a table

Chapter 4

- Create footnotes
- Insert a cover page
- Add a comment
- Use Track Changes
- Accept changes

PRODUCTION ASSISTANTS

Capstone Exercises

You work as a production assistant in the offices of a new company, the Green Man Theatre. You have been asked to create a press packet for Paul's Kitchen, *a Green Man production. The packet will include a cover page, a cover letter, a press release, and a brochure advertising upcoming Green Man productions.*

Create a Cover Page

You create a cover page for the press packet that introduces the *Paul's Kitchen* production and includes the date of the packet release and your name as the contact person for further information. You include the Green Man logo on the cover page and all other materials in the press packet for quick visual recognition.

a. Open *01w_PressPacket*, and then save it as **01w_Press Packet_LastFirst**.

b. Turn on **Show/Hide (¶)** to help you work with the multiple sections you will be creating for the press packet.

c. Set the document margins to **Normal**.

d. Insert a cover page in the **Semaphore** style. Change the document theme to **Facet**.

e. Type **Paul's Kitchen Press Release** as the document title. Type **Presented by Green Man Theatre** as the document subtitle.

f. Enter today's date using the Date Control. Remove the text box that contains the Author, Company name, and Address content controls.

g. Press **Ctrl+Home** to move the insertion point to the first paragraph mark at the top of the page. Press **Enter** twice and insert a **Sideline Quote box**. Type the following contact information using your e-mail address for the requested e-mail address.
Your name
Production Assistant
Green Man Theatre
Phone: 1 (612) 555-1212
Fax: 1 (612) 444-2323
E-mail:

h. Place the insertion point at the paragraph mark below the date. Insert the *01w_gmlogo* file and apply the **Square text wrapping style**. Apply **Align Middle** and **Align Center** to move the logo image down on the page.

i. Create a WordArt object on the cover page using the WordArt style **Fill - Dark Green, Accent 2, Outline - Accent 2** and **Green Man Theatre** as the text. Change the Font to **Times New Roman**, change the Text Fill color to **Green, Accent 1, Darker 25%**, change the Text Outline color to **Red**, and then select the Shadow style named **Offset Diagonal Top Left**. Apply the **Square text wrapping style** and move the WordArt to appear above the logo with text not overlapping the image. Apply **Align Center** to the WordArt.

Create a Cover Letter

You write a cover letter to members of the press inviting them to the *Paul's Kitchen* production and offering them four complimentary tickets.

a. Place the insertion point on the first line of the second page and insert a page break to add a blank page between the cover and press release pages. You will create a cover letter on this blank page.

b. Place the insertion point on the blank page before the page break.

c. Type a return address block using the following information.
Green Man Theatre
123 Main Street
Minneapolis, MN 55404

d. Insert three blank lines after the return address and add a date that will automatically update. Use the Month, Day, Year format.

e. Press **Enter** four times, type **Greetings Members of the Press:** as a salutation line, and then press **Enter** two times.

f. Write the text of the cover letter making sure there is **6 pt** spacing before and after each paragraph you create. Include the following information:

- An announcement that Green Man Theatre's 2016–2017 season is opening with a production of *Paul's Kitchen*, the story of seven friends, one van, and lots of laughs.

- The press will find the following information in the press packet:
  - Press release
  - Ticket price list
  - Brochure

- The press member is personally invited to enjoy a performance of *Paul's Kitchen*. The press member needs to present the press packet at the box office to receive their four complimentary tickets.

g. Insert a complimentary closing line followed by a comma.

h. Leave three blank lines after the complimentary closing line, type your name, and then press **Enter**.

i. Type **Production Assistant** as your title on the next line following your name.

j. Insert the **Grid header** to the cover letter. (*Note:* If the header text is not capitalized correctly, correct the title content control on the cover page.) Delete the Date Control. Add a **Bottom Border** to the header. Copy the logo from the cover page and paste it into the header. Resize the logo and use an appropriate wrapping style so that it fits attractively above the border line.

k. Add a **Semaphore footer**. Replace the page number text with the theater's contact information displayed in three lines with no space before paragraphs:
123 Main Street, Minneapolis, MN 55404
(612) 555-1212 www.greenman-theatre.com

l. Set the **Footer from Bottom distance** to **0.5"** in each section. Add a **Top Border** to the footer. Close the header and footer.

m. Change the page layout so that its vertical alignment is set to center.

Modify the Press Release

The basic information for the press release is on page 3 of the packet but needs to be formatted professionally. You format the press release.

a. Apply the **Emphasis style** to the text *Press Release* on page 3 of the press packet.

b. Change the style of the text *Green Man Theatre Announces the Opening of Paul's Kitchen* to the **Title style**.

c. Apply the **Intense Emphasis style** to the paragraph that begins *Paul's Kitchen opens. …*

d. Change the style of the line that begins *Minneapolis …* to the **Emphasis style**.

e. Move the insertion point to the second blank line following the paragraph that introduces the playwright and actors, and describes the basic plot of the play. Type **Tickets are available at the box office or online at:** and press **Enter**.

f. Press **Tab** and type the following address information on the next three lines, adding a tab at the beginning of the second and third lines:

Green Man Theatre
123 Main Street, Minneapolis, MN 55404
(612) 555-1212

Convert the Showtimes Table

To make the showtimes of *Paul's Kitchen* easier to read, you apply a table format that matches the theme you used on the cover page.

a. Convert the text listing dates and showtimes to a two-column table.

b. Format the table using the **Grid Table 5 Dark - Accent 2 table style**.

c. Adjust the left edge of the table so it aligns with the paragraph text preceding it.

d. Adjust the width of the first column so that the month and the day are not split.

e. Change the row height to **0.3"**.

f. Align the text in the table cells so that the text is centered vertically and aligned to the left side of the cells.

g. AutoFit the table content.

h. Center the table horizontally on the page.

Create a New Ticket Price List

You add a table to the press packet that displays the ticket types available and the costs per type of ticket. You format the table to match the theme colors.

a. Insert a **Page Break** after the table for a blank page.

b. Create a table with four columns and four rows.

c. Format the table using the **Grid Table 5 Dark - Accent 2 table style**.

d. Merge the cells of the top row, type the title **Green Man Theatre Ticket Price List** in the merged cell, apply the **Title style** to the title, and then center the title.

e. Type the following headings in the second row and first column:

Ticket Type	At the Door	Advance Purchase	Season Tickets
Adult			
Senior			

f. Insert a row above the *Adult* row and type **Student** as the *Ticket Type*.

g. Enter the *At the Door* ticket prices as shown:

Student	$15
Adult	$50
Senior	$25

h. Enter formulas with $ number format in the table to calculate these discounts:

- A 20% discount for all advance purchase tickets.

- A 25% discount for season tickets. The season ticket price is the equivalent of purchasing tickets to all three productions.

i. Apply the **Normal Style** to all rows of text below the title and change the font size to **14 pt**.

j. Set the table preferred width to **6.65"**.

k. Add a footnote to the Advance Purchase column heading: **Advance Purchase tickets receive a 20% discount and must be purchased at least two weeks before the show.**

l. Add a footnote to the Season Tickets column heading: **Season tickets receive a 25% discount. All three tickets of the season must be purchased at once to qualify for season ticket pricing.**

m. Press **Enter** twice for spacing between the footnotes and *footer* section. Place the insertion point below the ticket price table and press **Enter**.

Insert a Merchandise Price List

The Theater Shop manager asked you to include a price list of merchandise in the press packet. You create a link to the file containing these prices. The link will update the press packet information if there are any price changes in the Theater Shop.

a. Open the file *01w_PriceList*, copy the price list table, and then use Paste Special to paste link the table beneath the *Green Man Theater Ticket Price List*. Ensure that the link is in HTML format and that it will update if there are any price changes in the Theater Shop price list document.

b. Format the table using the **List Table 4 - Accent 2 table style**.

c. Apply the **Title style** to the table title and center the title. Change the font size to **10 pt** in the rows below the title.

d. Apply **Align Center Left** to the Items column and apply **Align Center** to the Price and Patron Discounts columns.

e. Adjust row heights to ensure that both tables fit on one page, if necessary.

f. Update a price in the *01w_PriceList* document to check to see if the copy/paste special was done correctly.

g. Close the file *01w_PriceList*.

Complete a Document Review

You proofread the press packet and note that some of the references to Green Man Theatre use *Theater* in the name instead of *Theatre*. After proofreading, you review the document by checking the spelling and grammar of each page. Finally, before presenting the press packet to the Board of Directors for approval, you add a question to the Board.

a. Turn on **Track Changes**.

b. Find all occurrences of *Theater* within *Green Man Theater* and replace with **Theatre** so that the company name is *Green Man Theatre*.

c. Check the spelling and grammar of the packet. Accept all references to *showtimes* as the correct spelling.

d. Accept all changes in the packet.

e. Select the phrase *four complimentary tickets* in the cover letter and add a comment: **Did we decide on two tickets or four tickets?**

f. Save and close the file. Submit files based on your instructor's directions.

Use Microsoft Excel

Background

Green Man Theatre is a local production company that puts on productions of plays and musicals. It has a small staff that takes care of production details, such as finances, scheduling, auditions, and so on. Community actors audition for roles in plays and are paid a small stipend. A production assistant uses spreadsheets to prepare budgets for current and upcoming plays and musicals, as well as prepare rehearsal schedules for current shows and financial reports based on past shows. Therefore, it is imperative that theater production assistants are proficient in using Microsoft Excel.

Tasks

The theater production assistant may be responsible for creating and maintaining spreadsheets for many purposes, including the following:

- Budget for upcoming shows
- Budget reports for previous shows
- Charts to represent revenue or ticket sales
- Mileage reimbursement

Skills

A production assistant should be able to do the following:

Chapter 1

- Enter and edit cell data
- Enter dates
- Use cell references in formulas
- Apply the order of precedence
- Copy formulas with Auto Fill
- Manage worksheets

- Manage columns and rows
- Apply alignment and font options
- Apply number formats
- Set page orientation
- Create headers and footers

Chapter 2

- Use relative, absolute, and mixed cell references in formulas
- Calculate a total with the SUM function
- Insert basic statistical functions
- Insert the TODAY function
- Determine results with the IF function
- Use LOOKUP function
- Use the PMT function

Chapter 3

- Select data source for a chart
- Choose a chart type
- Create a pie chart
- Move a chart
- Apply a chart style

Chapter 4

- Sort data
- Freeze panes
- Create a table
- Apply a table style
- Create a custom sort
- Apply text filter
- Apply conditional formatting

Capstone Exercises

You work as a production assistant for the Green Man Theatre. The director of operations asked that you prepare a packet to include an audition schedule and a budget for the upcoming show, Paul's Kitchen. In addition, she asked you to update the budget for the current show and create a chart. Finally, you need to create a forecast of ticket sales based on past shows. Rehearsals run for four weeks, starting Monday, August 1, 2016. The show opens Friday, September 9, 2016, just after the Labor Day weekend.

Complete a Proposed Budget for *Paul's Kitchen*

You need to compile data to create a proposed budget for *Paul's Kitchen*, the first show of the Green Man Theatre's 2016 season. The workbook contains some of the weekly salary and expense data you have already received from the director, stage manager, prop master, costume designer, and tech crew. You need to enter and format some data and calculate total weekly expenses and categorical totals for the two-month period.

a. Open *01e_Theatre* and save it as **01e_Theatre_LastFirst**.

b. Rename *Sheet1* **Budget Kitchen**. This sheet contains the proposed budget for the production of *Paul's Kitchen*.

c. Enter a function in **cell A2** that displays the current date each time you open the workbook.

d. Format the title *Budget for Paul's Kitchen* so that it is centered across columns A:K with **Calibri 16 pt font**. Apply the **Accent1 cell style** and adjust the row height to **23**. Align the text so that it is centered between the top and bottom of the cell.

e. Format the **range A3:K18** using **Calibri 12 pt**. Center and bold the column labels in **cells B3:K3**. Widen columns as needed.

f. Insert a row above cell A4 and enter the text **Salaries** in **cell A4**. Indent the row labels in **cells A5:A15** to categorize these rows as salaried positions.

g. Insert a row above cell A16 and enter the text **Other Expenses** in **cell A16** at the left margin and not indented as the cells above. Indent the row labels in **cells A17:A19** to categorize these rows as other expenses.

h. Enter data for salaries in **cells B6:J7**. The actors' salaries are $1,500 per week, and the stage manager earns $200 per week.

i. Format the **range B5:K20** with **Accounting Number Format** and with no decimal places. Adjust column widths as needed.

j. Insert a function in **cell K5** to calculate the total nine-week salary for the director. Use the fill handle to copy the function to **cell K19** and then delete everything from **cell K16**.

k. Calculate the weekly total expenses in **cell B20**. Copy the formula for the rest of the totals on row 20.

l. Apply the **Total Row cell style** to the **range A20:K20** and adjust the column width of column K as needed.

m. Save the workbook.

Calculate Projected Revenue and Net Profit

The bottom section of the Budget Kitchen worksheet contains Projected Ticket Sales. This section contains ticket prices by group and projected number of advance and door ticket sales. Green Man Theatre gives a 20% discount for tickets purchased in advance. You need to insert cells to make room for the advanced sales price per group and calculate the projected revenue.

a. Merge and center the title across the **range A23:F23**. Use Format Painter to copy formatting from **cell A1** to **cell A23**.

b. Type **Advance Discount** in **cell G24** and bold the label. Type **.25** in **cell G25**. Apply **Percent Style** with no decimal places.

c. Insert cells in the **range C24:C27** by shifting the existing cells to the right. Type **Advance Sales Price** in **cell C24**.

d. Format the labels in the **range B24:H24** with wrap text, bold, and centering.

e. Use the data in the **range B25:J25** and create a formula that calculates the advance purchase price for the Senior Citizens group. The formula should subtract the discount rate from 1 and multiply that difference by the contents of **cell B25**. Copy this formula to Adults and Students.

f. Enter a formula in **cell F25** that calculates total ticket revenue for projected senior citizen ticket sales. Copy the formula for the other two groups.

g. Calculate the total projected number of advance and door tickets sold in **cells D28** and **E28**, respectively. Calculate the total projected ticket sale revenue in **cell F28** and format with **Accounting Number Format**.

h. Apply a **Total Row cell style** to the **range A28:F28**.

i. Merge and center the **range A30:B30**. Use Format Painter to copy the formats from **cell A23** to **cell A30**.

j. Enter a formula in **cell B31** that displays the total projected ticket sales revenue that is stored in cell F28.

k. Enter a formula in **cell B32** that displays the total expenses that is stored in cell K20.

l. Enter a formula in **cell B33** that calculates the total profit after expenses.

m. Check for column width and consistent no-decimal formats. Revise cell formats as needed.

n. Apply **landscape orientation**. Create a footer that displays your name on the left side, the sheet tab code in the center, and the file name code on the right side.

o. Save the workbook.

Use the IF Function

Because actors work as independent contractors, they are reimbursed for mileage. The Green Man Theatre has an optional equal mileage payment plan that cast members can opt into to reduce the amount of paperwork. You have collected each of their round trip distances to the theater and have created an equalized mileage reimbursement based on whether they participate in the Mileage Payment Plan or not. The actors opting out of the equal mileage payment plan will turn in expense reports including their mileage logs and will receive mileage reimbursement in a lump sum at the end of the production based on their mileage logs.

a. Display the contents on the Mileage sheet.

b. Create a formula in **cell B7** to calculate miles driven by Ellen Anderson for all rehearsals and performances. The total number of rehearsals and performances is stored in cell B12. Use relative and absolute cell references appropriately. Copy the formula for the rest of the cast.

c. Create a formula in **cell B8** to calculate the total mileage reimbursement for Ellen Anderson. The reimbursement rate is stored in cell B11. Use relative and absolute cell references appropriately. Copy the formula for the rest of the cast.

d. Create an IF function in **cell B9** that equally divides the total mileage payments across the weekly pay periods for the production cycle of the show if the cast member opts into the Mileage Equal Payment Plan. If the cast member does not participate in the Mileage Equal Payment Plan, the function returns 0. The number of weeks of the production cycle is in cell B13. Use relative and absolute cell references appropriately. Copy this function for the rest of the cast.

e. Save the workbook.

Prepare Mileage Statistics

To help accurately prepare budgets for future productions, you prepare statistics on mileage expense reimbursement for each production. Because the number of actors varies from production to production, you need statistics on mileage reimbursement for a single actor.

a. Enter a function in **cell B16** to calculate the minimum total mileage reimbursement.

b. Enter a function in **cell B17** to calculate the maximum total mileage reimbursement.

c. Enter a function in **cell B18** to calculate the average total mileage reimbursement.

d. Enter a function in **cell B19** to calculate the total mileage reimbursement.

e. Apply **landscape orientation**.

f. Save the workbook.

Calculate a Loan Payment

Part of your responsibility in managing the budget is to make recommendations on loan expenses. The Board of Directors has voted to replace the sound system and take out a loan to finance the cost. A theater patron is the president of a local bank. She has guaranteed an interest rate of 4.25% on a five-year loan for the sound system. The board approved the purchase of an $18,995 sound system, including installation. How much will the monthly payment be on the loan?

a. Display the contents of the Sound System worksheet.

b. Enter the input values in **column B**, as mentioned in the above paragraph. Green Man Theatre will make monthly payments, so type **12** for the number of payments in one year.

c. Insert a **PMT function** in **cell B6** to calculate the monthly payment. Be sure the result displays as a positive number.

d. Save the workbook.

Use a Lookup Function

The Green Man Theatre has created an Honor Circle to thank their most generous patrons. The required donations for each level in the Honor Circle are listed in the table below. One of your responsibilities is to keep track of patrons' donations and give them appropriate acknowledgements in the play bill. You will use a lookup function to assign the appropriate Honor Level to your Patrons list. You will then apply conditional formatting to the table to highlight Silver members to be targeted for additional donations next year. To ensure Platinum members are recognized on the program, you will filter the list.

Platinum	$10,000
Gold	$1,000
Silver	$100

a. Display the contents of the Patrons worksheet.

b. Create a lookup table starting in **cell G3** using the above table. Make sure the data is organized appropriately for a lookup table.

c. Apply **Accounting Number Format** to the values and **General format** for the text. Assign a range name **Honor_Lookup** to the lookup table.

d. Create a **VLOOKUP function** in **cell D3** that returns the honor level based on each patron's gift.

e. Copy this function for the rest of the patrons.

f. Select the **range A2:D43** and convert it to a table. Apply the **Table Style Light 9 style**.

g. Freeze the header row so the column headings will always be visible.

h. Create a custom sort list to sort the table by Honor Level so Platinum patrons are at the top of the list, then by Gold, and finally Silver. Sort the patrons alphabetically by last name inside the Honor Level groupings.

i. Apply conditional formatting to the table to highlight members that donated between $700 and $1,000 using **Green Fill with Dark Text** as the highlighting color.

j. Filter the Patrons table to display only the Platinum members.

k. Save the workbook.

Create a Budget Summary

After a successful run of *Paul's Kitchen*, you create a budget summary and graphs summarizing ticket sales. Remarkably enough, the production stayed on budget and Green Man Theatre's ticket sales projections were pretty accurate.

a. Copy the Budget Kitchen worksheet and rename the copied sheet **Budget Summary**. Move the Budget Summary sheet after the Mileage worksheet.

b. Change the header for the *Projected Ticket Sales* section to **Ticket Sales**. Because *Paul's Kitchen* came in on budget, you do not need to make any changes to the budget section.

c. Enter these ticket sales numbers as your final sales figures, replacing the projected figures:

Ticket Type	At-Door Seats	Advance Purchase Seats
Senior	84	252
Adult	163	604
Student	111	72

d. Use the final sales figures to construct two pie charts on this sheet to compare the percentage of ticket types. The first chart should show percentage by ticket type of advance tickets sold. The second chart should show the percentage by ticket type of tickets sold at the door. Position the first chart so the top-left corner is in or near **cell M4** and the second chart should have its top-left corner in or near **cell M23** and size the charts as necessary.

e. Apply **Chart Style 3** to both charts to include chart titles, legends, and data labels showing percentages. Replace the text **Chart Title** with an appropriate title for each chart.

f. Save and close the workbook. Submit based on your instructor's directions.

Use Microsoft Access

Background

In order to store and analyze the data for a theater company, production assistants might use Microsoft Access. They create and maintain tables, create and edit queries, and create forms and reports. Theater data includes shows, theaters, actors, and casting. Producers and directors will use this data to determine which actors performed in which shows, which theaters were used more frequently, and which shows were profitable.

Tasks

In a theater company's business office, a production assistant might be asked to create and maintain many types of database objects, including the following:

- Tables
- Queries
- Forms
- Reports

Skills

A production assistant should be able to do the following:

Chapter 1

- Open an Access file and work with content security
- Navigate among the objects in an Access database
- Edit a record
- Save the database
- Back up, compact, and repair an Access file
- Sort table data on one or more fields
- Use the Relationships window
- Understand relational power
- Enforce referential integrity

Chapter 2

- Create tables
- Set a table's primary key
- Work with field properties
- Import an Excel spreadsheet
- Establish table relationships
- Create a single-table query
- Use Query Design view
- Specify query criteria for different data types
- Run, copy, and modify a query
- Create a multi-table query
- Modify a multi-table query

Chapter 3

- Create a calculated field in a query
- Create expressions with Expression Builder
- Format and save calculated results
- Verify calculated results
- Use built-in functions in Access
- Perform date arithmetic
- Add aggregate functions to datasheets and queries
- Create a totals query with grouping

Chapter 4

- Create forms using the Form tool
- Modify a form
- Revise forms using Layout view
- Identify control types in forms
- Create reports using the Report Wizard
- Preview a report
- Modify a report
- Revise reports using Layout and Design views
- Identify control types in reports

PRODUCTION ASSISTANTS

Capstone Exercises

You work as a production assistant in the office of the Green Man Theatre. One of your duties is to maintain the company database. You will create and edit tables, queries, forms, and reports as well as maintain and back up the database. A database has already been created, so you decide to explore it.

Navigate Among the Objects in an Access Database

Open the Broadway database and examine the tables and other objects. You will also make one change in the Actors table.

a. Open the database *01a_Broadway*. If a Security Warning message bar appears, enable the content and continue. Save the database as **01a_Broadway_LastFirst**.

b. Open each table and examine the data.

c. Close all the tables except the Actors table.

d. Sort the Actors table by Last Name in ascending order.

e. Find Stacie Henderson's record.

f. Replace the last name *Henderson* with **Tandbell**.

g. Remove the Sort.

h. Save and close the Actors table.

i. Open the *Actors from NY* query.

j. Switch to Design view. Modify the State criterion so the query displays all the actors who are not from NY.

k. Save the query (use save object as) and rename as **Actors Not from NY**. Close the query.

Create a Casting Table

The database contains tables for theaters, shows, and actors. However, there is no efficient way to keep track of which actors performed in which shows. You will create a Casting table that will contain the show, the actor, and the weekly pay.

a. Create a table using Table Design.

b. Add field names and data types as listed below.

Field Name	Data Type
ShowID	Number
ActorID	Number
WeeklyPay	Currency

c. Set ShowID and the ActorID together as the primary key.

d. Save the table as **Casting** and close the table.

Import Excel Data into the Casting Table

The theater has been storing casting data in an Excel spreadsheet. You will import this spreadsheet data directly into the Casting table.

a. Append the data in Sheet1 of the *01a_ImportCasting* Excel file into the Casting table.

b. Open the Casting table and examine the data.

c. Verify the primary key is set correctly by changing the last record's ActorID from *12* to **9**. Click the record directly above and Access will display the message *The changes you requested to the table were not successful …* Undo the change to ActorID.

d. Close the table.

Establish Table Relationships

Table relationships help users extract data more efficiently. Referential integrity will help eliminate common data entry mistakes. You will set two new relationships and enforce referential integrity.

a. Open the Relationships window and add the Actors and Casting tables.

b. Set a relationship between the Shows and Casting tables and set Enforce Referential Integrity.

c. Set a relationship between the Actors and Casting tables and set Enforce Referential Integrity.

d. Make sure all table data and join lines are visible.

e. Save and close the Relationships window.

Create a Casting Query

You need to post the casting roll for each new show. You will create a casting role for the latest show using a query.

a. Create a query based on the Casting table. Include only the ShowID and ActorID fields.

b. Add criteria to display all the actors who performed in ShowID 3, which is *Jersey Boys*.

c. Run the query.

d. Save the query as **Jersey Boys Cast**.

e. Close the query.

Copy and Modify an Existing Query

The previous query does not show the name of the show or the name of the actor. You will copy the previous query and revise it to add the missing data.

a. Copy the Jersey Boys Cast query and paste it using the name **Jersey Boys Cast Enhanced**. Open the Jersey Boys Cast Enhanced query in Design view.

b. Add the Actors and Shows tables into the new query.

c. Modify the query so that the ShowName displays as the first column and the ShowID field does not display in the query results.

d. Replace the ActorID field with the LastName and FirstName fields.

e. Run the query. Verify the accuracy of the data.

f. Save and close the query.

Use a Calculated Field to Forecast Daily Revenue

The producers have asked you for the daily estimated revenue for each show, based on a sold-out house. You will create a query and use a calculated field to provide this information.

a. Create a new query based on the Shows and Theaters tables.

b. Include the ShowName, TheaterName, SeatingCapacity, and TicketPrice fields.

c. Save the query as **Estimated Daily Revenue**.

d. Use the Expression Builder to create the DailyRevenue calculated field in the fifth column. Multiply the field Seating-Capacity by TicketPrice to create the calculated field.

e. Close the Expression Builder, run the query, and then manually verify whether the calculated field values are correct.

f. Save and close the query.

Use Functions in a Query

The producers ask you to modify and improve the Estimated Daily Revenue query. You will copy the existing query, rename it, and then add the required changes. The new query will require a Totals query so you can look up the total actors' salaries for each show.

a. Create a Totals query from the Casting table that can be used to look up the total actors' salaries for each show. Add the ShowID and WeeklyPay fields. Use the Total row to group by ShowID and sum the WeeklyPay. Run the query and save the query as **Show Salaries**. Close the query.

b. Copy the Estimated Daily Revenue query and paste it using the name **Estimated Daily Revenue and Expenses**.

c. Modify the *Estimated Daily Revenue and Expenses* query to add a Daily Rent calculated field to the sixth column using **DailyRent: [WeekRentalFee]/7**. Change the format property to **Currency**. Run the query and verify whether the calculated field is working.

d. Switch to **Design view** and add a **Daily Salaries calculated field** to the seventh column using the expression: **DailySala-ries: DLookUp("SumOfWeeklyPay," "Show Salaries," "Sho-wID= " & [ShowID])/7**.

   The DLookup() function directs Access to look up a value in the Show Salaries query you created in step a. Change the format property to **Currency**.

e. Run the query and manually verify whether the calculated field values are correct. Save and close the query.

f. Copy the *Estimated Daily Revenue and Expenses* query and paste it using the name **Estimated Net Income**. Add another calculated field for **Daily Net**. Daily Net is defined as Revenue minus Expenses. Add another calculated field for **Total Net**. Total Net is defined as Daily Net times the number of days the show runs. Total Net requires the DateDiff() function, as shown: **Total Net: [Daily Net]*DateDiff("d,"[StartDate], [EndDate])**.

g. Run the query and verify the calculated fields are correct.

h. Save and close the query.

Create a Form Using a Form Tool

You need to create a form to make it easier to add new actors. The same form will function as a maintenance screen for existing actors.

a. Create a form based on the Actors table using the Form tool.

b. Resize the width of the text box controls so they are about half the original size.

c. Remove the subform.

d. Change the title label to **Enter and Edit Actor Data**.

e. Save the form as **Maintain Actors**.

f. Add yourself as an actor using the new form. Include your real name and make up the rest of the data.

g. Close the form.

Create a Report Using the Report Wizard

You need to create a report that lists all the actors grouped by show. The report should also show the weekly pay for each actor and a sum for each show, as well as display a sum for the weekly pay overall.

a. Create a simple query that will be used to create a report. Include the Casting, Shows, and Actors tables. Add the necessary fields based on the description above.

b. Name the query **Casting Summary**. Close the query.

c. Create a report based on the Casting Summary query using the Report Wizard. Answer the Report Wizard's questions using the description above. Name the report **Casting Pay by Show**.

d. Switch to **Layout view** and delete the summary for the Show-Name box displayed in the ShowName footer. Preview the report.

e. Switch to **Design view** and move the Sum label and Sum box up to the top of the ShowName footer. Reduce the height of the ShowName footer by one-half. Preview the report.

f. Save the report. Close the report.

g. Add yourself as ActorID 20 to the Jersey Boys show in the Casting table and preview the report again.

h. Close the report.

Compact, Repair, and Back Up the Database

An Access database needs to be maintained regularly. As a part of your daily routine, you will compact, repair, and back up the database.

a. Compact and repair the database.

b. Back up the database in the location where you save your student files. When naming the file, include today's date.

c. Save and close all open database objects, and submit the database based on your instructor's directions.

Use Microsoft PowerPoint

Background

Microsoft PowerPoint can be a powerful tool for use in a theater company's business office. Production assistants use PowerPoint to create presentations, handouts, and scripts for presentations. It is important that a production assistant become familiar with planning a presentation, creating text, inserting media, and working with transitions and animation to utilize the benefits of this program. The following presentation skills are crucial to people employed as production assistants.

Tasks

In a theater company's business office, a production assistant might be asked to create and develop many types of presentations. Tasks involving PowerPoint could include:

- Planning and creating presentations centered upon a theme
- Preparing progress report presentations
- Creating advertisements and flyers
- Preparing process SmartArt diagrams
- Printing handouts for crews

Skills

Production assistants should be able to do the following:

Chapter 1

- Use PowerPoint views
- Create a new presentation
- Edit the title slide
- Add new slides
- Use spell check
- Reorder slides
- Insert a media object
- Add a table
- Animate objects
- Apply transitions
- Use slide layouts
- Apply themes

Chapter 2

- Add pictures
- Import an outline
- Reuse slides from an existing presentation

Chapter 3

- Use a callout shape
- Change a shape outline
- Create SmartArt
- Modify SmartArt
- Create WordArt
- Modify WordArt
- Modify objects
- Group objects
- Arrange objects

Chapter 4

- Insert a picture
- Transform a picture
- Remove a picture background
- Add audio
- Change audio settings

Capstone Exercises

You work as a production assistant in the offices of a new company, the Green Man Theatre. You have been asked to create a presentation to display in a kiosk in the theater shop and box office to advertise season tickets.

Create a Title Slide

You create a title slide for the new presentation, and then you insert audio to catch the attention of viewers.

a. Create a new blank PowerPoint slide show and save it as **01p_Season_LastFirst**.

b. Apply the **Facet theme**. Format the background style to apply the **Canvas texture** to this slide and all other slides.

c. Add the title **GREEN MAN THEATRE** in the **title placeholder**. Select the title and apply WordArt **Gradient Fill–Orange, Accent 4, Outline-Accent 4**. Resize the title font to **60 pt**.

d. Type **2016–2017 Season** in the **subtitle field** of the title slide. Change the font to **White, Background 1** and bold. Resize the subtitle font to **40 pt**.

e. Insert the Green Man Theatre logo, *01p_gmlogo.jpg*. Remove the white background from the logo and resize the logo to a height **4.3"** and a width **4.41"**.

f. Position the logo in the top-right corner of the slide.

g. Insert the *01p_gmaudio* audio file on Slide 1. Set the playback options to play the audio across slides and hide the icon during the show. Position the audio icon on the bottom-left side of the slide.

h. Apply the **Start After Previous animation option** to the audio icon.

i. Apply the following **entrance animations** and review the presentation to ensure the animation is correct:

Object	Animation	Start	Duration	Delay
Title placeholder	Grow & Turn	With Previous	04.00	18.00
Subtitle placeholder	Swivel	With Previous	03.00	03.00
Logo image	Bounce	With Previous	06.00	10.00

Create a Mission Statement

You add a new slide for the mission statement, type content in the placeholders, format the text, and then reposition the placeholders.

a. Insert a new slide using the **Content with Caption layout**.

b. Type **Mission Statement** in the **title placeholder** and change the font size to **54 pt**.

c. Type **Green Man Theatre** in the **text placeholder** below the title and change the font color to **Orange, Accent 4**. Change the font size to **32 pt**.

d. Add the following mission statement to the **content placeholder**:

We are committed to providing the environment and the resources for new artists, musicians, actors, and dancers to create and perform new works in the Twin Cities.

e. Change the font size of the text in the content placeholder to **30 pt**. Adjust the position of the placeholder so that the bullet symbol is aligned across from the title text and remove the bullet formatting.

Create a Title Slide

You insert a new slide, add and format a table, insert a logo, add a callout object, and then apply an animation.

a. Insert a new slide using the **Title and Slide Content layout**. Title it **Green Man Theatre Presents**. Change the title text color to **Orange, Accent 4**.

b. Insert a two-column by four-row table on the slide. Enter the following information:

Show	Dates
Paul's Kitchen	September 9–October 2, 2016
Christmas at the Andersons'	November 25–December 18, 2016
This Was Not in the Brochure	February 23–March 19, 2017

c. Apply the **Light Style 2–Accent 4 table style** to the table and adjust the column widths and row heights so that no text in cells is split into two lines, if necessary.

d. Copy the logo from the Title slide and paste it on Slide 3. Resize the logo to height **3.45"** and width **3.54"**. Center-align the logo at the bottom edge of the slide.

e. Create an **Oval Callout shape** to the right of the logo and type **2016–2017 Season** in the callout. Format the callout style to **Colored Outline–Orange, Accent 4**.

f. Position the callout so it is associated with the logo image and move the callout point so that it appears to come from the logo man's mouth. Group the logo and the callout as shown in Figure 1.1.

g. Apply a **Float In entrance animation** with **Float Down effects** to the **title placeholder**, having it start **After Previous**. Copy the animation to the logo group and then to the table.

FIGURE 1.1

Add Existing Content to a Presentation

You have an outline describing two of the three plays of the season in a Word file. You also have the start of a slide show about the third play. You use this existing content to add the show descriptions to the presentation you are creating.

a. Use the *Slides from Outline* feature to add both slides contained in the *01p_Outline* file to the end of *01p_Season_LastFirst*.

b. Add a slide at the end of the presentation by reusing the slide in *01p_Brochure.pptx*.

c. Use Format Painter to apply the format from the content on Slide 2 to Slides 4–6 and copy the format from the title on Slide 3 to Slides 4–6.

d. Modify the outline in Outline view by moving the bullets referring to the show running dates so they are the first bullet in each of the new Slides 4–6.

e. Photographs in your student data files are named *01p_Paul's_Kitchen_1*, *01p_Paul's_Kitchen_2*, *01p_Christmas_at_the_Andersons'*, and *01p_This_Was_Not_in_the_Brochure*. Insert these photos on the appropriate slides.

f. Position the images attractively on the slides.

g. Format each of the photos by removing backgrounds, applying color corrections, adjusting color, applying filters, and/or adding picture styles.

h. Insert a new slide after Slide 6 using the *Content with Caption* layout.

i. Add the title **Season Tickets** and change the font size to **44 pt**. Type **Green Man Theatre** in the **text box** below the title and change the font color to **Orange, Accent 4**. Change the font size to **32 pt**.

j. Add these bullets in the **content box**:

   - **Available in the Box Office and Theater Shop**
   - **Discount on Season Tickets**
   - **Patron Memberships Available**

k. Change the content text size to **32 pt** and apply **12 pt** after to the line spacing.

l. Copy the logo image from the first slide and resize and position the logo below the slide's title.

Create SmartArt

You create a SmartArt diagram to explain the three levels of giving and the amount required to achieve a particular level. Different benefits are available to patrons of different levels.

a. Insert a new slide after Slide 7 using the Title Only layout.

b. Type **Patronage Levels** in the **title placeholder** and format the text to match the other titles in the presentation.

c. Create a **Pyramid List SmartArt** to display three levels of giving.

   - Platinum $10,000
   - Gold $1,000
   - Silver $100

d. Change the color of the SmartArt style to **Colorful Range–Accent Colors 2 to 3**.

e. Apply the **Cartoon SmartArt 3-D style**.

f. Display the slides in Slide Sorter view and move Slide 8 (Patronage Levels) behind Slide 2 (Mission Statement).

g. Apply the **Reveal transition effect** for all slides.

Finalize the Presentation

You apply final animations to the presentation, and then prepare the presentation to play automatically at the kiosk located at the entrance to the theater.

a. Apply a consistent entrance animation of your choice to all bulleted content placeholders in the presentation. The bullets should enter one by one.

b. Apply an animation to the SmartArt on Slide 3 that wipes the objects from the left and one by one.

c. Apply an animation of your choice to each of the images you inserted on the slides introducing the plays.

d. Check for spelling or grammar errors.

e. View the presentation and make any changes necessary.

f. Save the presentation. Submit based on your instructor's directions.

g. Save the presentation again as **01p_Kiosk_LastFirst**.

h. Set up the slide show so it can be browsed at a kiosk. Set the slide show to use slide timings.

i. Use the Rehearse Timings feature to add automatic slide timings to advance each of the slides in the presentation. Figure 1.2 shows sample times for each slide.

j. Save and close the file, and submit based on your instructor's directions.

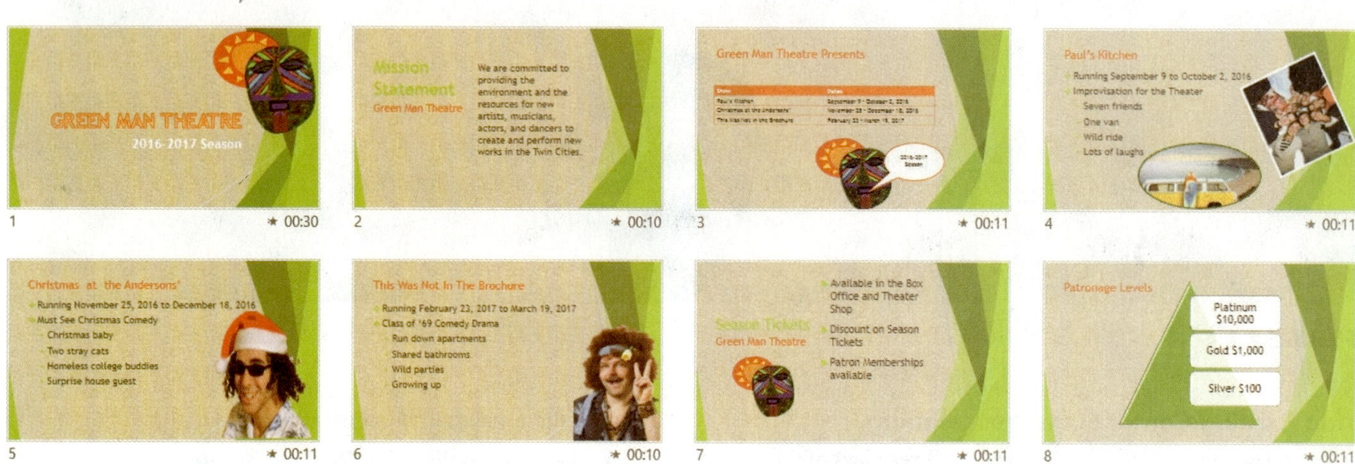

FIGURE 1.2

Integrate Microsoft Office Software

Background

Each program in the Microsoft Office suite has its strength and specialty. The theater production office assistant needs to use each software program in the suite for the appropriate task. Microsoft Word is useful to create fliers and brochures for upcoming plays and musicals, letters to send to patrons and donors, and so on. Microsoft Excel is appropriate to store budgets for the current and upcoming productions and to develop schedules and reimbursement forms that require mathematical calculations. Microsoft PowerPoint is beneficial for creating presentations for advertising the productions or when meeting with investors. Microsoft Access is a database management program that provides the capability to store and analyze large quantities of data. At times, the production office assistant needs to use all four programs together to create the desired result. For example, the production assistant may use data from Access to generate an Excel workbook for further data analysis and then create a chart that can then be linked to a PowerPoint presentation shared with the theater board members as a PDF file.

Tasks

In a theater company's business office, a production assistant might be asked to find data and present information using all the applications in Microsoft Office 2013. This could include the following:

- Create handouts in Word for a board meeting
- Calculate basic sales summary statistics in Excel
- Export data from Access database queries to Excel for quantitative manipulation
- Link data and charts from Excel into PowerPoint presentations

Skills

In addition to basic formatting skills, a production office assistant should be able to do the following:

- Create a summary query
- Export query results to an Excel worksheet
- Calculate statistics using MIN, MAX, and AVERAGE functions
- Create charts from data
- Display the statistics and charts as linked objects in a PowerPoint presentation
- Share the presentation as an e-mail PDF attachment

PRODUCTION ASSISTANTS

Capstone Exercises

You work as a production office assistant in the offices for the Green Man Theatre. You maintain the season tickets database. Your job entails creating and executing queries to help the production manager make critical decisions about the theater's operations. At times, you need to export Access data into an Excel worksheet for other data manipulations, create charts in Excel that you can import into a PowerPoint presentation, and import data into Word documents for distribution.

Export Queries to Excel

The sales manager asks you to create a query to determine how many seats each season ticket holder owns for the opening weekend and then import the results into an Excel workbook so he can analyze sales. You will export the tables and a few queries for just the opening weekend to a test database so you do not accidentally change any of the data in the actual database. If this becomes a regular function, you will move the queries into the actual database. Season tickets are sold by the seat. Each show has its own set of seats. The tables of seats for each show are the following:

Table	Show
Show1	Opening Friday Night
Show2	Opening Saturday Night
Show3	Opening Sunday Matinee

a. Open the Access database *01i_SeasonTickets.accdb* and save it as **01i_SeasonTickets_LastFirst**.

b. Create a query for Friday night using the Show1 table and the SeasonTicketHolders table. Insert the fields in the following sequence: CustomerNum from the Show1 table, LastName and FirstName from the SeasonTicketHolders table, and Seat from the Show1 table. Group by CustomerNum and create a calculated field to count the number of seats each ticket holder owns for opening Friday night. Customize the column labels using the Property Sheet to display **Seat Number** instead of *Seat* and **Customer Number** instead of *CustomerNum*. Save the query as **SeatCount1**.

c. Repeat step b above, replacing Show2 and Show3 for Show1 and naming the queries **SeatCount2** and **SeatCount3**, respectively.

d. Close Access and submit the database based on your instructor's directions.

e. Open Excel and create a blank workbook. Import data from the three queries created above into the Excel workbook. In the **Select Table dialog box**, check the box to enable selection of multiple tables. Next, select the option to view the data as a table in the workbook.

f. Delete Sheet1, which is blank. Rename each worksheet tab with data according to the show number in the last column. For example, Sheet2 will be renamed to *Show1*.

g. Save the Excel workbook as **01i_SeatCount_LastFirst** and keep the file open for the next steps.

Perform Statistics Calculations on Imported Data in Excel

After you give the workbook to the sales manager, he comes by your office and admits he does not know what to do with it. He asks if you could do some analysis on the buying habits of the season ticket holders. He wants you to create a summary area in which you perform statistical calculations on each worksheet's data. For each show, he wants to know the total number of seats sold and the number of ticket holders, along with the maximum, minimum, and average number of seats purchased by each ticket holder.

a. Set the first sheet, Show1, as the active sheet. Press and hold **Shift** as you click the **Show3 tab** to group the three sheets together. Anything you do now will affect all the grouped sheets.

b. Click **cell H1**, type **Sales Statistics for Opening Friday Night**, and then press **Enter**. Bold the label and apply the **Accent6 cell style**.

c. Start in **cell H2** and type the following labels down the column:

- **Total seats sold**
- **Number of ticket holders**
- **Maximum number of seats purchased**
- **Minimum number of seats purchased**
- **Average number of seats purchased**

d. Apply **merge and center** to the **range H1:I1**. Adjust the width of column H to best fit the remaining labels.

e. Enter functions in column I for each respective label.

f. Select **cell I6**, apply **Comma Style**, and then display one decimal place.

g. Click the second worksheet tab to ungroup the sheets.

h. Review each function on the other two worksheets and adjust the ranges within the function arguments as needed for each particular sheet of data. In **cell H1** for the other two worksheets, replace *Friday Night* with **Saturday Night** and **Sunday Matinee**, respectively.

i. Save the workbook and keep it open.

Create a Summary Chart

The sales manager wants you to create a column chart that depicts the total number of season tickets sold by opening night. You will consolidate the data on a new worksheet in order to be able to create a column chart.

a. Insert a new worksheet in front of Show, and name it **Summary**.

b. Type **Summary** in **cell A1** and press **Enter** twice.

c. Type **Friday Night**, **Saturday Night**, and **Sunday Matinee**, respectively, in the **range A3:A5**. Widen the column so text is visible.

d. Click **cell B3**, type =, click the **Show1 sheet tab**, click the cell containing the total seats sold function, and then press **Enter**.

e. Adapt step d to create formulas that point to the original respective functions for Saturday and Sunday.

f. Create a column chart on the Summary sheet by using the Summary data. Add an appropriate chart title, add data labels, and then increase the font size of the data labels to **12 pt**.

g. Move the chart below the data to cover the **range B8:I29**. Click in any cell to deselect the chart.

h. Save the workbook and keep it open.

Link Data into a PowerPoint Presentation

The sales manager is pleased with the statistical analysis and chart you added to the Excel workbook. He decides to use the summary data and chart in a PowerPoint presentation that he can show at the next board meeting. You will create a presentation with a title slide, the three summary statistical tables on one slide, and the chart on a third slide.

a. Start PowerPoint and select the **Main Event design template**. Apply the green shaded variants to the design. Save the presentation as **01i_Stats_LastFirst**.

b. Type **Green Man Theatre** in the **title placeholder** and type **Opening Night Ticket Sales** in the **subtitle placeholder** on the title slide.

c. Insert a second slide using the Title Only layout and do the following:

- Type **Summary Statistics per Show** as the title.
- Copy the Summary Statistics for Opening Friday Night range on the Show1 sheet from the *01i_SeatCount_LastFirst* workbook and use Paste Special to paste a link onto the slide.
- Copy the Summary Statistics for Opening Saturday Night range on the Show2 sheet from the *01i_SeatCount_LastFirst* workbook below the first linked range on the slide.
- Copy the Summary Statistics for Opening Sunday Matinee range on the Show3 sheet from the *01i_SeatCount_LastFirst* workbook below the second linked range on the slide.
- Increase the width of each summary area object and arrange them to be centered under the title.

d. Insert a third slide, using the Blank layout. Copy and link the column chart from the workbook onto the slide. Using the top-left corner of the image, drag it to toward the top-left edge of the slide to enlarge it, and then apply align center.

e. Save the presentation and keep it open.

Share the Presentation

Finally, after you prepare the presentation, the sales manager asks you to create a PDF of the presentation to e-mail to the board of directors before the meeting.

a. Use the Share feature in PowerPoint to e-mail your instructor a PDF attachment of the presentation.

b. Replace the file name with **Green Man Theatre - Summary Statistics** as the e-mail subject.

c. Type a brief message to encourage the recipient to open and review the attached presentation file.

d. Send the e-mail message.

e. Exit all open programs.

f. Submit based on your instructor's directions.

Business Discipline

Using Microsoft Office as a Business Professional

BACKGROUND | Working as a Business Professional

A career in business involves a variety of communication and analytical skills. You will also often be required to communicate through written documents, and you will most likely need to make and deliver presentations. In many areas of business you might also need to organize and analyze data.

The Microsoft Office suite of applications provides tools that are critical in helping the business professionals from office assistants to CEOs with whatever task is required. For example, you would use Word to write letters, memos, reports, brochures, or newsletters. With PowerPoint you can design presentations or even flyers to communicate information to your customers or stakeholders. You could be required to analyze financial or sales data using Excel. Finally, Access can help you to capture and store sales and other customer-related data and then filter and sort that data into meaningful information that can then be used by others in your company.

Discipline-Specific Capstones

Using Office in the Business Profession

Application	Exercises	Skills Covered

1. WORD
   Data Files:
   02w_AnnualLetter
   02w_Bike1.jpg
   02w_Bike2.jpg
   02w_Bike3.jpg
   02w_Bike4.jpg
   02w_CoverLetter
   02w_Dataset
 	
   Solution Files:
   02w_AnnualLetter_Solution
   02w_CoverLetter_Solution
   02w_MergedLetters_Solution
	WRITE THE ANNUAL LETTER (page 27)	• Set margins • Insert a watermark • Insert a footer • Format a footer • Insert a cover page • Replace an image • Resize an image • Change document theme • Add text to content controls on a cover page • Use Track Changes • View and delete a comment • Accept/Reject changes • Convert text to a table • Insert a row • Adjust row height • Acknowledge a source • Create footnotes • Insert a symbol • Apply a table style • Adjust table position and alignment • Format table text • Calculate using table formulas • Check spelling and grammar • Insert nonbreaking space • Modify document properties • Add page numbers • Modify paragraph spacing • Select indents • Apply styles • Use WordArt • Complete a mail merge • Use a data source

2. EXCEL
   Data Files:
   02e_Budget
   02e_Image1.jpg
 	
   Solution Files:
   02e_Budget_Solution
	MODIFY A FINANCIAL STATEMENT (page 30)	• Design a worksheet • Rename a worksheet • Change tab color • Copy a worksheet • Enter and edit cell data • Insert columns and rows • Adjust column width • Insert a date function • Create a footer • Insert an image into a cell • Merge and center labels • Apply alignment and font options • Apply cell styles • Apply number formats • Use cell references in a formula • Use relative and absolute cell references • Use AutoSum • Copy formulas with AutoFill • Apply conditional formatting • Select a range and assign a name • Use a range • Use the VLOOKUP function • Use the PMT function • Select the data source • Create column and pie charts • Insert sparklines • Move a chart • Apply a chart layout and a chart style • Format data labels • Create a table • Apply a table style • Apply a number filter • Hide and unhide columns and rows • Display cell formulas • Set page orientation • Set margin options

Project	Project Title	Skills
3. ACCESS Data Files: 02a_Motorcycles 02a_ProductCategory.xlsx Solution Files: 02a_Motorcycles_Solution	**MANAGE A COMPANY DATABASE (page 33)**	• Navigate among the objects in an Access database • Add and edit records • Sort table data on one or more fields • Use and remove a filter • Understand relational power • Use the Relationships window • Understand and establish table relationships • Enforce referential integrity • Create a database • Design a table • Create and modify tables • Import an Excel worksheet • Create a single-table query • Use query design view • Specify criteria in a query for different data types • Run, copy, and modify a query • Create a multi-table query • Modify a multi-table query • Create a calculated field in a query • Format and save calculated results • Verify calculated results • Create expressions with the Expression Builder• Use built-in functions in Access • Create a totals query with grouping • Create a form using form tools • Modify a form • Enter data in Form view • Create reports using the Report Wizard • Modify a report • Revise reports using Layout and Design views • Change column width in report • Preview reports in Print Preview • Back up, compact, and repair Access files
4. POWERPOINT Data Files: 02p_BusOutline.docx 02p_Draft 02p_Figure1.jpg 02p_Figure2.jpg 02p_Figure3.jpg 02p_Figure4.jpg Solution Files: 02p_BusOutline_Solution.rtf 02p_MotorcycleSafety_Solution 02p_MotorcycleSafety_Solution.ppsx	**REACH OUT TO THE COMMUNITY (page 37)**	• Modify an outline in Word • Create a new presentation • Import an outline and reuse slides • Use slide layouts • Add new slides • Insert images • Resize and apply picture effects to images • Add speaker note • Add a table • Format a table • Apply themes • Add a graphic image • Format text as WordArt • Use the Internet as a resource • Insert an audio clip • Insert a video clip • Use transitions and animations • Run and navigate a slide show • Save presentation as a PowerPoint Show
5. INTEGRATED Data Files: 02i_HealthyLiving.accdb 02i_IncomeStatement.xlsx 02i_Newsletter.docx 02i_Outline.rtf 02i_Shareholders.xlsx Solution Files: 02i_HealthyLiving_Solution.accdb 02i_Finance_Solution.pptx 02i_Finance_Solution.ppsx 02i_IncomeStatement_Solution.xlsx 02i_MergedMemo_Solution.docx 02i_Newsletter_Solution.docx 02i_VaShareholders_Solution.xlsx	**INVITE TO THE ANNUAL MEETING (page 40)**	• Import an Excel worksheet into Access • Create and utilize a database containing contact information • Use the Input Mask Wizard • Export an Excel worksheet from Access • Format a worksheet • Create formulas using cell references and absolute references • Apply theme • Rename worksheet • Change tab color • Merge and center labels • Apply cell styles • Insert a date function • Create a footer • Create a chart in Excel • Apply a chart layout and a chart style • Use WordArt • Set page orientation • Set margin options • Insert watermark • Create sections in Word • Apply and modify headings • Insert a worksheet into a Word document • Insert a footnote, footer, and hyperlinks • Complete a mail merge • Use a data source • Create a presentation file • Import an outline • Format slides • Insert and format a chart • Add animation • Create a PowerPoint Show

Use Microsoft Word

Background

Companies place office managers and directors in charge of various departments, which include accounting, finance, human resources, marketing, manufacturing and production, public relations, and research and development. These upper management employees are responsible for planning and supervising the work of their subordinates and for achieving the organizational goals so that the company is successful. Office managers use word processing software on a daily basis to prepare correspondences, record notes, and prepare reports and proposals. Although e-mail and messaging have replaced some written correspondence, office managers still often use word processing software to prepare written documents. The following word processing skills taught in the textbook are crucial skills needed by people employed in management.

Tasks

Office managers may be responsible for all kinds of document production. Such documents could include the following:

- Correspondence and mailings
- Contracts
- Mailing lists
- Tables
- Brochures, flyers, and pamphlets
- Forms and reports
- Requests for proposals

Skills

In addition to basic formatting skills, office managers should be able to do the following:

Chapter 1

- Begin and edit a document
- Customize Word
- Use features that improve readability
- View a document in different ways
- Prepare a document for distribution
- Modify document properties

Chapter 2

- Apply font attributes
- Format a paragraph
- Format a document
- Apply styles
- Insert and format objects

Chapter 3

- Insert a table
- Format a table
- Manage table data
- Enhance table data
- Create a Mail Merge document
- Complete a Mail Merge

Chapter 4

- Use a writing style and acknowledge sources
- Create and modify footnotes and endnotes
- Explore special features
- Review a document
- Track changes

Capstone Exercises

You work as the assistant director of the Public Relations department of Healthy Living Motorcycles, Inc. Your company will be holding its annual meeting soon, and you are responsible for mailing the invitational letter and accompanying materials to the shareholders. Your executive assistant had collected the necessary information and written a draft for you. You will review the draft and add your changes and suggestions to the annual letter to shareholders. In addition, you will draft a cover letter to accompany the annual letter and to provide more information about the annual meeting.

Set Initial Document Formats

It is important to format documents for easier readability and to conform to company requirements. You will change the margins, format the character and spacing, and insert a watermark. You also want the page number and the company name to appear in the footer of every page.

a. Open *02w_AnnualLetter* and save it as **02w_AnnualLetter_ LastFirst**.

b. Set the margin setting to **Normal**.

c. Select the entire document and set the paragraph Line spacing option to **Single**, Spacing After option to **6 pt**, Alignment option to **Justified**, and font type and size to **Times New Roman, 11 pt**.

d. Include the word *DRAFT* in a semitransparent, diagonal watermark.

e. Insert the **Integral style** footer. Type **your full name** in the **Author text field**. The page number appears after the typed text.

f. Format the footer using **Times New Roman, 10 pt**.

Insert a Cover Page

You want the document to look professional and eye-catching, so you add a "colorful" image to the cover page to make it more interesting.

a. Insert a cover page at the beginning of the document using the **Integral** design. Replace the image with the **02w_Bike1.jpg** file. Increase the height of the image to **2.5"**.

b. Change the document theme to **Integral**.

c. Change the document title to **Annual Letter**. Change the font to **Times New Roman, bold**, and shrink the font by one size.

d. Type **Healthy Living Motorcycles, Inc.** as the document subtitle.

e. Change the abstract title to **To Our Shareholders**. Change the font to **Times New Roman, bold**, and increase the font by one size.

f. Type **Our Motto: We are committed to global sustainability and social responsibility.** in the Abstract content control.

g. Change the author's name to **your full name** and the font type to **Times New Roman**. Type **Assistant Director of Public Relations** in the Course content control.

Review a Document Using Track Changes

Your executive assistant added several comments in the document. After reviewing the document, you incorporate the changes in the document and remove all comments and highlighting.

a. Change the Display for Review options to All Markup to display all comments.

b. Insert **2015** before the text Net Sales Performance as indicated in the second comment.

c. Delete all three comments and change the Display for Review options to No Markup.

Convert Text to a Table and Format Table

Your executive assistant was not sure how to format the net sales information. You decide that putting the sales figures in a table will make it easier for shareholders to understand.

a. Move to the 2015 Net Sales Performance section. Select all the text starting with **Countries** and ending with -**5.8**. Convert the selected text to a table. Use two columns and separate text by tabs. Delete any empty rows, if necessary. Change the column width of the first column to **1.8"** and the second column to **3"**. Select the whole table and change the row height to .**3"**.

b. Insert one row at the top of the newly created table. Merge the cells in the first new row. Change the row height to **0.4"**. Cut and paste the text **2015 Net Sales Performance** located above the table into the merged cell. Insert a footnote at the end of the table title. Add the footnote text: **Source: Healthy Living Annual Report, 2015**. Insert the **copyright symbol** at the end of the sentence.

c. Apply the **Grid Table 4 – Accent 2 Table Styles** to the table.

d. Select the whole table and set the paragraph Spacing After option to **0 pt** and the cell alignment to **Align Center Left**. **Center** the table horizontally on the page.

e. Set the alignment to **Align Center** in the first row.

f. Bold the 2015 Net Sales % Change column heading in the second row.

g. The countries are listed under two continents: Asia and Europe. Indent all the countries under each continent by **0.5"** and sort the countries in ascending order within each continent.

h. **Bold** and **right-align** the total percentages for Asia and Europe.

i. Create a caption to display above the table. Type **A Comparison of Two Years' Sales** as the caption for the table. Center the caption and change the font type to **Times New Roman, 11 pt**.

Insert and Format Graphics

You want to showcase the four new inventions strategically on the third page of the document.

a. Insert a page break right before the *Four Latest Innovative Products* heading.

b. Format the *Four Latest Innovative Products* heading as Heading 1. Modify Heading 1's font type to **Times New Roman**, **Bold**, and the paragraph Spacing After option to **12 pt**.

c. Place the insertion point before *Sports Motorcycle # 1* and insert a two-columns-by-two-rows table. Set the cell height to **2.5"** and cell width to **3.25"**.

d. Navigate to your Student Data folder, and insert the **02w_Bike1.jpg** image in the cell of row 1 column 1, **02w_Bike2.jpg** in the cell of row 1 column 2, **02w_Bike3.jpg** image in the cell of row 2 column 1, and **02w_Bike4.jpg** in the cell of row 2 column 2.

e. Scale the height of all four images to **2"** and set the images to **Align Top Center**.

f. Create a caption for each figure by cutting and pasting the motorcycle information listed in the document and place the caption below the image.

g. Center the caption. Center the table and remove all the borders of the table.

h. Insert a page break to force the paragraph below the graphics onto a new page.

i. Select the text starting with Chairman, President, and CEO to VP – Global Outreach on the fourth page, and format it with the Multilevel List. Use any bullet images of your own choosing.

j. Apply the Heading 1 format to the *Thank You for Your Support and Faith in Us* heading.

Prepare the Document for Sharing and Change Document Properties

Before sending the final document to your director for her approval, you will check for misspellings, remove widows or orphans, and insert nonbreaking spaces if necessary.

a. Use the Spelling & Grammar tool to check the annual letter for errors and correct all misspelled words.

b. Proofread the document and correct any errors you identify.

c. Change the view to Read Mode and scan the document to ensure there are no widows or orphans. Change back to Print Layout view. Make sure that the document is only four pages long.

d. Set the document's advanced properties with the following information (the first three should be set already):

- The Author is **your full name**.
- The Title is **Annual Letter**.
- The Subject is **Healthy Living Motorcycles, Inc.**
- Keywords are **motorcycles, bikes, sustainability, environmental- friendly**.

e. Save and close the document.

Modify the Cover Letter

Your executive assistant used an existing standard company letter template to write the cover letter, so you simply have to change some of the information in the letter instead of having to create a new one. However, you need to make sure that all personal information, such as names and addresses, is correct.

a. *Open 02w_CoverLetter*, and save it as **02w_CoverLetter_LastFirst**.

b. Format the document as follows:

- Set the margin setting to **Normal**.
- Select the entire document, and set the Line spacing option to **Single**, paragraph Spacing Before and After options to **6 pt**, Alignment option to **Justified**, and font type and size to **Times New Roman, 11 pt**.

c. Insert **four** blank lines at the beginning of the document.

d. Use the **WordArt Fill – Blue, Accent 1, Shadow style, font size 28** to insert **Healthy Living Motorcycles, Inc.,** and center it across the top of the letter.

e. Start a Mail Merge using the Step-by-Step Mail Merge Wizard. Use the current letter as the starting document, and the recipient information is derived from *02w_Dataset*.

f. Replace the bracketed placeholders in the letter, *Address Block*, *First Name*, and *Email Address*, with fields from the data source. Use default settings for the Address block. Set the paragraph Spacing After for Address Block to **0 pt**.

g. Replace the bracketed placeholders in the letter, *Student Full Name* and *Student Email Address*, with your own full name and email address.

h. Complete the merge, merging all records with the data source, resulting in three letters. Save the merged letters as *02w_MergedLetters_LastFirst*.

i. Ensure that the letter prints on one page. Save and close the documents.

j. Submit all the files based on your instructor's directions.

Use Microsoft Excel

Background

Employees in the accounting and finance departments find worksheet software such as Microsoft Office Excel indispensable. Worksheets give employees the ability to manipulate data to prepare budgets and financial statements. This is particularly useful in "what-if" analysis, where a change in one number in the worksheet can result in updates to all formulas associated with that specified cell reference. The following worksheet skills are crucial skills needed by employees in all business functions.

Tasks

Office managers may be responsible for creating and maintaining many types of worksheets. These worksheets could include the following:

- Revenue and expense sheets
- Budgets
- Financial statements
- Payroll documents
- Information from vendors and clients

Skills

In addition to basic formatting skills, office managers should be able to do the following:

Chapter 1

- Explore the Excel window
- Enter and edit cell data
- Create formulas
- Use AutoFill
- Display cell formulas
- Manage worksheets
- Manage columns and rows
- Select, move, copy, and paste data
- Apply alignment and font options
- Apply number formats
- Select page setup options
- Preview and print a worksheet

Chapter 2

- Use relative, absolute, and mixed cell references in formulas
- Insert a function
- Insert basic math and statistics functions
- Use date functions
- Use LOOKUP functions
- Calculate payments with the PMT function
- Create and maintain range names
- Use range names in formulas

Chapter 3

- Select the data source
- Choose a chart type
- Move, size, and print a chart
- Add chart elements
- Format chart elements
- Apply a chart style and colors
- Modify the data source
- Create and customize sparklines

Chapter 4

- Freeze rows and columns
- Print large datasets
- Design and create tables
- Apply a table style
- Sort data
- Filter data
- Use structured references and a total row
- Apply conditional formatting
- Create a new rule

Capstone Exercises

You are the assistant director of the Accounting and Finance depart-ments at Healthy Living Motorcycles, Inc. In addition to ensuring that all daily business transactions are completed accurately, you also play a key role in assembling the annual financial reports. Currently, you are responsible for putting together the financial statements to be presented to the upcoming Annual Stockholders Meeting.

Enter and Format Identifying Information

Your executive assistant has collected all the financial statements from the various departments and assembled them into a basic workbook. You will expand on the workbook to include informa-tion that would be helpful to you. To give it a professional look, you insert the company image and format the company informa-tion at the top of the worksheet. To keep track of the changes, you add your name and the date at the bottom of the worksheet.

a. Open *02e_Budget* and save it as **02e_Budget_LastFirst**.

b. Rename the first worksheet to **Selling & Admin Expenses** and change the sheet tab color to **Red**.

c. Change the font to **Arial** for the entire worksheet.

d. Insert a blank row below Total Selling Expenses (row 10) and below Total Administrative Expenses (row 17). Use an appro-priate date function in **cell A29** to display today's date in your worksheet. Use the **Short Date format**, apply **bold**, and set the font size to **12 pt**.

e. Type your first name and last name in **cell A30**.

f. Create a footer with your **full name** on the left side, the **Sheet Name** in the center, and the **File Name** on the right side of the worksheet.

Format Column Labels and Data

Some of the column labels in the worksheet overlap each other and are not completely displayed. To make the worksheet more professional-looking, you want to format the column labels and widths.

a. Move the content in **cells A1:A3** to **B1:B3**. Merge the range **A1:A3** and insert *02e_Image1.jpg* into the merged cell. Adjust the height of the image to **1"** and center it in the cell.

b. Merge, center, and apply **Heading 1 Cell Styles** to the **range B1:G1**. Increase the font size by **1**. Select the **Gold, Accent 4, Darker 50% font color**. Apply the **Gold, Accent 4, Lighter 80% fill color**.

c. Merge, center, and apply **Heading 2 Cell Styles** to the range **B2:G2**. Increase the font size by **1**. Select the **Gold, Accent 4, Darker 25% font color**. Apply the **Gold, Accent 4, Lighter 60% fill color**.

d. Merge, center, and apply **Heading 3 Cell Styles** to the range **B3:G3**. Put "and Five Year Projections" on the next line.

Increase the font size by **1**. Select the **Gold, Accent 4, Darker 50% font color**. Apply the **Gold, Accent 4, Lighter 40% fill color**.

e. Merge, center, and apply **Heading 1 Cell Styles** to the range **B5:G5**.

f. Apply **Heading 2 Cell Styles** to the range **B6:G6**. Increase the font size to **14 pt**.

g. Apply the **Total Cell Styles** to range **A19:G19**. Increase the font size for A19 to **16 pt**. Change column size of Column A to **41 pt**.

h. Apply **Heading 1 Cell Styles** to cells **A7** and **A12**.

i. Apply **Heading 2 Cell Styles** to cells **A10** and **A17**. Indent both headings **3 times**.

j. Format the range **B8:G19** with **Accounting Number Format with no decimal places**.

k. Format the range **B22:B27** with **percentage** and **one decimal place**.

l. If necessary, adjust all row heights as needed so that all head-ings are visibly displayed.

Use AutoSum and Absolute References

Employees frequently need summarized information to make good business decisions and future projections. You also want to apply conditional formatting to emphasize values above the aver-age value.

a. Use **AutoSum** for the year of 2015 to find the total selling expenses in **cell B10** and the total administrative expenses in **cell B17**.

b. Create a formula in **cell B19** that adds the total selling and administrative expenses.

c. Use both **absolute references** and **relative references** to reflect the percentages in cell range A22:B27 to determine the pro-jected expenses for each of the Budgeted Selling and Budgeted Administrative Expenses for the year of **2016**.

d. Use AutoFill to complete the series in **ranges D8:G17** and **C19:G19**.

e. Apply the **Light Red Fill with Dark Red Text conditional for-matting** to values in the Total Selling Expenses row when the values are above $10 million.

Assign a Range Name and Use a VLOOKUP and PMT Function

Next, you will proceed to create a range name and insert finan-cial functions into the worksheet. Due to the expansion into the global markets, the board of directors is considering the purchase of a new factory. The board would like to consider the options of financing the purchase over a period of 10 to 40 years, depending on the interest rates and monthly payments. You will present various financing options to the board. The terms and corresponding interest rates are stored in a lookup table. You will assign a range name to the lookup table so that you can use the range name in a function. You will then use the VLOOKUP and PMT functions to determine the monthly payment for the purchase.

a. Assign the range name **Rates** to the **range D2:E10** on the Factory worksheet. Change the tab color of the worksheet to **yellow**.

b. Create a VLOOKUP function in **cell B6** that looks up the loan period in **cell B5**, compares it to the Rates Lookup table, and then returns the corresponding interest rate. Use the range name for the VLOOKUP function. Change the loan periods to perform several "what if" analyses to determine the interest rates for the corresponding loan terms.

c. Create the **PMT** function in **cell B7** to determine the monthly payment based on the financed amount, the loan period, and the corresponding interest rate in range **B4:B6**. Ensure that the monthly payment is a positive number.

d. Format the **financed amount** and **monthly payment** as **currency with no decimal place**, and all the **interest rates** as **percentage with 2 decimal places**. Apply **Top and Double Bottom border** to cell B7.

Create Sparklines and Insert a Chart

Executives are very busy and often prefer to view summarized data using charts. You use a column chart to illustrate the projected selling and administrative expenses for the next five years, but you also insert sparklines to display spending trends for the total selling and administrative expenses. Finally, you use a pie chart to compare the percentages of the various expenses for 2015.

a. Move to the Selling & Admin Expenses worksheet. Create a 3D Clustered Column chart in a new worksheet based on the **ranges A6:G6, A8:G9, and A13:G16** for the five years' projections.

b. Apply the **Layout 5 Chart Styles** to the column chart to display the data table at the bottom on the chart. Insert the chart title as **Five Years' Projection** and increase the chart title font size to **28**.

c. Move the tab with the 3D Clustered Chart to the right of the Selling & Administrative Expenses worksheet tab. Name this tab as **3D Clustered Chart** and change the tab color to **Blue, Accent 1, Darker, 50%**.

d. Click the Selling & Admin Expenses tab and insert a Line sparkline in **cell H10** for the total selling expenses and a Column sparkline in **cell H17** for the total administrative expenses. Custom the Market Color for both low points in **red** and the high points in **green**.

e. Create a 2D pie chart for the year of 2015 using the labels and data in **ranges A8:B9 and A13:B16**.

f. Move the chart to a new chart sheet named **Pie Chart**, and to the right of the **3D Clustered Chart** sheet. Change the tab color of the Pie Chart sheet to **Purple**.

g. Type the chart title as **Selling and Administrative Expenses for 2015**. Apply the **Style 9 Chart Styles** to the pie chart to display the percentages and category names outside each slice. Increase the chart title font size to **28**.

h. Explode the largest slice and insert a block arrow with the text. This is the largest portion pointing to the largest section of the pie chart. Resize the block arrow to display the whole text.

Create and Format a Table

You want to convert the data in the Selling & Admin Expense worksheet to a table and use Excel's table features to continue working with the data. Since you also want to preserve the original worksheet, you want to first create a copy of the worksheet. After you convert a copied data set to a table, you will format it with a table style. You also want to *hide* one column and freeze the column labels so that they do not scroll off screen.

a. Copy the Selling & Administrative Expenses worksheet and place the copy after the original worksheet. Rename the copied sheet as **Selling & Admin Table**. Change the tab color of the new sheet to **Green**.

b. Select the **range A6:G19**, and convert the data to a table.

c. Remove the conditional formatting rule. Apply the **Table Style Light 21 table style**.

d. Apply **Green, Accent 6, Darker 50% font color** to the **range B6:G6** to coordinate the font color with the table color.

e. Hide **Column B** (2015) to display only five years' projection.

f. Display the formula to ensure that all formulas are correct. Protect the current sheet without a password, allowing users to select locked and unlocked cells.

Format and Save the Workbook

a. Correct and remove any green triangle arrow if necessary.

b. Change the orientation for the Selling & Admin Expenses and Selling & Admin Table tabs to **landscape**. To fit the Selling & Admin Expenses tab to one page, change the margin to **Narrow**, the bottom margin to **.5"**, and the width of Column A to **38**. Preview the workbook to make sure that all the individual worksheets fit on one page. If necessary, fit the whole worksheet onto one page.

c. Save and close the workbook. Submit based on your instructor's directions.

Use Microsoft Access

Background

Employees use database management software such as Access to maintain and manipulate data for business reasons. The Information Systems (IS) department is primarily responsible for creating and maintaining the databases to be used by all employees in the organization. Database software gives employees the ability to manipulate data to provide output needed to prepare reports and correspondences. The following database skills taught in the textbook are crucial skills needed by people employed in management.

Tasks

Employees may be responsible for creating and maintaining database information. This information could include the following:

- Tables
- Queries
- Forms
- Reports

Skills

Employees should be able to do the following:

Chapter 1

- Understand database fundamentals
- Use an existing database
- Sort table data on one or multiple fields
- Create, modify, and remove filters
- Know when to use Access or Excel to manage data
- Understand relational power
- Create a database

Chapter 2

- Design a table
- Create and modify tables
- Share data
- Establish table relationships
- Create a single-table query
- Specify query criteria for different data types
- Understand query sort order
- Run, copy, and modify a query
- Use the Query Wizard
- Create a multitable query
- Modify a multitable query

Chapter 3

- Create a calculated field in a query
- Format and save calculated results
- Create expressions with the Expression Builder
- Use built-in functions in Access
- Add aggregate functions to datasheets
- Create queries with aggregate functions

Chapter 4

- Create forms using form tools
- Use form views
- Work with a form layout control
- Sort records in a form
- Create reports using report tools
- Use report views
- Modify a report
- Sort records in a report

Capstone Exercises

You are the assistant director for the Information Technology (IT) department at Healthy Living Motorcycles, Inc. In addition to overseeing hardware and software selection, system maintenance, and employee IT training, you create and maintain databases for the whole organization. The organization uses one central database rather than maintaining several individuals ones to reduce data redundancy and errors. You will take the opportunity to create an efficient database to keep track of and manage information regarding the company's employees, customers, products, and shareholders.

Create a Table and Import Excel Data

You have an existing database that contains the products sold by the company. However, you need to create a table that will classify each product under a specific category. After the table is created, you import the category data into the newly created table.

a. Open the *02a_Motorcycles* file and save it as **02a_Motorcycles_ LastFirst**.

b. Import the data in the *02a_ProductCategory.xlsx* Excel file into a newly created table. Use the column headings from the Excel file, select the CategoryID field as the primary key, and then save the table as **Product Category**.

c. Modify the field properties as follows:

Field Name	Data Type	Field Size	Comments
CategoryID	Short Text	2	• Assigned a 2-letter code • Caption = Category ID • This is a required field • Set Indexed = Yes (No Duplicates) • Primary key
CategoryName	Short Text	25	• Caption = Category Name • This is a required field • Set Indexed = Yes (No Duplicates)
Description	Long Text		
SupplierID	Short Text	4	• Caption = Supplier ID • All Supplier ID must begin with an "S." • Set Indexed = No

d. View the data in the Product Category table in Datasheet view and adjust column widths so all data is visible.

e. Save and close the table.

Create Relationships

You are now ready to create relationships among the four tables (Employees, Product Category, Suppliers, and Products) so that you can make the database more efficient.

a. Create the following relationships and enforce referential integrity:

- Product Category and Suppliers tables using the Supplier field.
- Suppliers and Employees tables using the EmployeeID and EmployeeContactID fields.
- Product Category and Products tables using the CategoryID field.

b. Save and close the Relationships window.

Create Filters

You need to quickly find the products which were supplied by a foreign country. You will open the Suppliers table and filter the records.

a. Open the Suppliers table in Datasheet view.

b. Filter the records for the suppliers who were outside of the United States. You should have 11 records.

c. Close the table.

Create a Single-Table Query

The director of marketing has requested a list of the suppliers that have more than 25,000 square feet.

a. Create a query using the Suppliers table to display the SupplierID, SupplierName, and Capacity fields for those plants with more than 25,000 square feet. Sort the results by SupplierName in ascending order.

b. Run the query.

c. Name the query as **Supplier Size**.

d. Save and close the query.

Create a Multi-Table Query

The director of marketing wants a list of the employees who are the main contact with the suppliers. He also wants the addresses of these contact employees so that he can personally send them a letter thanking them for working diligently with these suppliers.

a. Create a query using the Suppliers and Employees tables.

- Display the SupplierName, EmployeeLastName, EmployeeFirstName, E_StreetAddress, E_City, E_State, and E_PostalCode fields. Sort the results by EmployeeLastName, in ascending order.

b. Run the query.

c. Save the query as **Contact Employee Address**.

d. Close the query.

Create a Query and a Date Arithmetic Calculated Field

The human resources manager would like a list of all employees and the approximate length of time they have worked for the company.

a. Create a query using the Employees table and include the EmployeeLastName, EmployeeFirstName, and Date_of_Hire fields.

b. Create an expression in the first blank column of the query that calculates the length of time, in years, employees have worked for the company, using the Date_of_Hire field and the current date. Do not adjust for days off. Name the expression **Tenure**. Format the Tenure field as **Fixed with 2 decimal places**.

c. Name the query as **Employee Tenure**.

d. Create a report from the Employee Tenure query.

- Group by Date_of_Hire—by Month.

- Sort ascending by Date_of_Hire.

- Change the title to **Employee Tenure Report**. Make sure all fields display appropriately.

e. Widen the columns to display all text. Save the report with the default name and close it.

Create a Query with a Profit Margin Calculated Field

The accounting manager works on the income statements and balance sheets, and he would like to know the profit margin for each product.

a. Create a query named **Profit Margin Per Unit**.

- Add ProductName, UnitPrice and UnitCost fields from the Products table.

- Use the Expression Builder in the first blank column of the query to create a calculated field named Profit Margin Per Unit to determine the profit margin for each unit.

- Format the UnitPrice, UnitCost, and Profit Margin Per Unit fields as **Currency with 2 decimal places**.

- Sort the query so that the highest profit margins are displayed at the top of the query. Run the query.

- Find the averages for the UnitPrice, UnitCost, and Profit Margin Per Unit columns.

- Save and close the query.

Create a Supplier Form

Your organization is always looking for more suppliers to manufacture products. You create a new form to make it easier to enter new supplier information.

a. Create a new form based on the Suppliers table using the Form tool.

b. Change the title label control to **Enter Supplier Information**.

c. Reduce the text box widths to one-half of their original size.

d. Change the form's control padding to **Narrow**.

e. Save the form as **Enter Supplier Information**.

f. Switch to Form view. Enter a new supplier record, **#15**, using the following information:

- SupplierID: **S115**

- SupplierName: **Student's University**

- Delete the content in EmployeeContactID.

- SupplierContactLastName: **Student Last Name**

- Supplier Contact Title: **Student**

- S_StreetAddress, S_City, S_State, S_Postal Code: **Student's school address**

- S_Country: **USA**

- Leave Capacity at 0 and leave the Home Page and ProductID fields blank.

g. Sort the form by SupplierName, ascending order.

h. Save and close the form.

Create a Report Using the Report Wizard

The director of marketing would like a report that lists the suppliers who manufacture the various motorcycles. You create the report for him using the Report Wizard.

a. Create a query and name it **Motorcycles by Suppliers**.

- Add the SupplierName, SupplierContactLastName, and Capacity fields from the Suppliers table.

- Add the ProductName and ProductSize fields from the Products table.

- Sort in descending order by Capacity.

- Run, save, and close the query.

b. Create a report based on the **Motorcycles by Suppliers** query.

- View the data by Suppliers, and group the data by SupplierName.

- Sort the data by ProductName, ascending order.

- Select **Landscape Orientation** for the report.

- Use **Block** layout.

- Save the report title as **Motorcycles Grouped by Suppliers**.

- Preview the report.

c. Change the column widths so all the data is visible. Widen the Report Header title control so the entire title is visible. Preview the report.

d. Switch to Print Preview and make sure that the report is displayed on one page. Exit Print Preview and close the report.

Create a Query and a Report with an Overtime Calculated Field

The director of accounting wants to know the cost of time-and-a-half overtime, over and above the regular payroll for all hourly employees in the organization. You need to create a query to find all the employees who worked overtime and then create a report based on the query results.

a. Create a query using the Employees table to calculate the hourly rate at time and a half for those employees who work more than 40 hours per week.

- Include the following fields: EmployeeFirstName, EmployeeLastName, Hours, Rate, and E_State.

- Calculate the weekly overtime costs in a column called **Weekly Overtime**. Please note: Only the hours worked over 40 hours per week count towards overtime pay. Format the field as **Currency with 2 decimal places**.

b. Name and save the query as **Weekly Overtime**.

c. Create a report for the Weekly Overtime query.

- Format the report with a title of **Employee Overtime** and all columns fit on one portrait layout page.

- Switch to Layout View and use the SUM function to calculate the total cost of overtime pay to all employees.

- Apply the **Organic theme** to the report.

- Change the report title to **Employee Weekly Overtime**, **bold** it, and then change Control Margins to **None**.

d. Preview the report and adjust column widths so that the content appears on one page.

e. Save the report as **Employee Overtime** and close the report.

Compact, Repair, and Back Up the Database

You compact the database to eliminate any unused space. You also back up the database and save it as another name.

a. Compact and repair the database.

b. Back up the database in the location where you save your student files. When naming the file, include today's date.

c. Submit the database based on your instructor's directions.

Use Microsoft PowerPoint

Background

Employees of business organizations use presentation software frequently to communicate with others on important topics. Microsoft PowerPoint makes it possible for the user to create presentations with media elements, charts and graphs, and transitions and animations. However, business employees must understand the features of PowerPoint and be comfortable using those features. The following presentation skills taught in the textbook are skills crucial to business employees.

Tasks

Office employees may be responsible for creating all types of presentations and documents using PowerPoint. These could include the following:

- Presentations to a board meeting
- Printed handouts for distribution to stakeholders such as customers, clients, and community members
- Informative presentations display at an exhibit or outreach program

Skills

Employees should be able to do the following:

Chapter 1

- Use PowerPoint views
- Type a speaker note
- Save as a slide show
- Plan a presentation
- Assess presentation content
- Review the presentation
- Insert media objects
- Add a table

- Use animations and transitions
- Insert a header or footer
- Run and navigate a slide show
- Print in PowerPoint

Chapter 2

- Create a presentation using a template
- Modify a presentation based on a template
- Create a presentation in Outline view
- Modify an outline structure
- Print an outline
- Import an outline
- Reuse slides from an existing presentation
- Modify a theme
- Modify the slide master

Chapter 3

- Create shapes
- Apply Quick Styles and customize shapes
- Create WordArt
- Modify WordArt
- Modify objects
- Arrange objects

Chapter 4

- Insert a picture
- Transform a picture
- Use the Internet as a resource
- Add video
- Use Video Tools
- Add audio
- Change audio settings

Capstone Exercises

You are the executive assistant to the director of Public Relations department at Healthy Living Motorcycles, Inc. As outreach to the community, the director has been asked to present to a local high school about motorcycle safety next week. He would like to educate students on how to stay safe on the roads, and he asked you to prepare the motorcycle safety PowerPoint slide show according to the following instructions.

Modify an Outline in Word

Your director has written an outline for the presentation in Microsoft Word and saved it as an .rtf (rich text format) file. You modify the outline before inserting it into a blank presentation.

a. Open the *02p_BusOutline.rtf* file in Word and save it as **02p_BusOutline_LastFirst**.

b. Add **AGENDA** as a Heading 1 item at the top of the document and then go to the end of the document and add **ANY QUESTIONS?** as the last Heading 1 item in the document.

c. Save and close the file.

Set Up the Slide Show

You create a presentation using a template, set up the title page, insert a header and footer, and apply a design and color theme to the document.

a. Start PowerPoint, and create a new presentation using the **Retrospect** template. Save the presentation as **02p_MotorcycleSafety_LastFirst**.

b. Enter the following text into the placeholders:

- Title placeholder: **MOTORCYCLE SAFETY**.
- Subtitle placeholder: **Presented By: Student First name Last name**.

c. Create a handout header with your full name, and a handout footer with your instructor's full name, and the course number and title. Include the current date to update automatically.

d. Change the theme to the **Ion theme**.

Import an Outline and Reuse Slides

Now you are ready to work on the material content of the presentation. You import the Word outline into the presentation. Your director has also created a basic slide show with speaker notes about motorcycle safety. For efficiency, you reuse this content in your slide show too.

a. Import the *02p_BusOutline_LastFirst.rtf* outline file into the presentation.

b. Add the following items at the end of the existing bullets on Slide 4:

- Treat other drivers with courtesy and respect
- Do not weave in and out of stalled traffic
- Obey all traffic laws

c. Go to Slide 8. Reuse Slides 2 through 4 from *02p_Draft*.

d. Switch to Notes Page view and copy the speaker note on Slide 9 to the title slide.

e. Apply **Push** transition effect to odd slides and **Wipe** transition effect to even slides.

f. View the slide show.

Insert Images and a Table

Although the slides contain important information, they look bland and boring. To make it more appealing to your audience, you decide to add several images to Slides 5–8. You also add a table to Slide 9 to tabulate some important data.

a. Insert the image *02p_Figure1.jpg* on Slide 5, *02p_Figure2.jpg* on Slide 6, *02p_Figure3.jpg* on Slide 7, and *02p_Figure4.jpg* on Slide 8.

b. Change the width of all four images to **5"** and center the images below the text.

c. Apply the following Picture Effects to the four images:

- The **Tight Reflection, touching Reflection style** to Figure 1.
- The **Dark Red, 18 pt glow, Accent Color 1** glow style to Figure 2.
- **Relaxed Inset** to Figure 3.
- The **Off Axis 1 Right 3-D Rotation** to Figure 4.

d. Adjust the placeholders on all four slides so that the images are positioned appropriately on the slides.

e. Insert a table with six rows and six columns on Slide 9.

- Enter the following information into the table cells:
- Center all cell content horizontally and vertically.
- Resize the table to a width of **10.5"** and position it attractively in the blank space.
- Apply the **Themed Style 1 – Accent 3 table style**.

Quarter	1st Quarter	2nd Quarter	3rd Quarter	4th Quarter	Total (Year)
2010	8,459	9,435	9,582	9,582	37,423
2011	7,552	8,975	8,252	8,252	33,883
2012	6,755	8,522	8,496	8,496	32,999
2013	6,708	8,216	8,483	8,483	32,367
2014	7,530	8,620	8,450	8,450	33,780

Add a Graphic Shape

Sometimes a graphic shape can be used to draw attention to a topic. You add shapes and WordArt to two slides to enhance the text. After adding the shape, you group it with another image to form an attention-grabbing graphic.

a. Insert the **Circular Arrow shape** (third row, third column in the *Block Arrow category*) on Slide 10.

b. Change the width of the shape to **3"** and the height to **4"**.

c. Rotate the arrow **Right 90°**, and position the arrow on the right so that the arrow head points towards the text placeholder.

d. Search the Internet for an image using the key word *motorcycle*.

e. Select an appropriate motorcycle image, and position it on top of the Circular Arrow shape. **Group** the motorcycle image and the Circular Arrow shape.

f. Select the grouped item and apply the **Metal Oval Picture Style**.

g. Change the layout to **Blank** on Slide 12. Highlight the *ANY QUESTIONS?* text, format it with the **Pattern Fill – Dark Red, Accent 1, 50%, Hard Shadow - Accent 1 WordArt**, and then center the WordArt on the slide.

Modify the Outline and Change Slide Layouts

To focus on the content of the presentation, you review the text in Outline view. You use the spell checker and make the necessary corrections. You hyperlink the URLs and modify the last slide.

a. Change to Outline view. Review the outline, and if necessary, remove any unnecessary blank lines in the outline.

b. Switch to Normal view. On Slide 11, format all references as bullets and hyperlink the URLs.

c. Copy and paste all the slide titles starting with Slide 3 as bullets onto Slide 2 Agenda to finalize the presentation.

Add Media Objects and Sound

You decide to add a video clip and an audio clip to catch your audience's attention.

a. Go to the title slide, search the Internet for an **audio clip** using the keyword *motorcycle*, select an appropriate audio clip, and insert it onto Slide 1. Start the sound automatically and hide the sound icon during the show. Loop the sound until stopped so it plays continuously until the next slide displays. Drag the sound icon to the bottom-left corner of the slide.

b. Use the Internet as a resource and search for a video on youtube.com using the key words *motorcycle safety*.

c. Copy and paste the name and URL of the selected video clip onto the text placeholder on Slide 10. Type a short speaker note on this slide about your video.

d. Add the **Applause sound** to signify the end of the presentation on the last slide. Hide the icon.

Add Animation

Now that the presentation has been created, add animations to introduce elements at appropriate times and to create visual interest.

a. Apply the **Entrance Split Effect, with Vertical In Effect Options** to the image on Slide 5.

b. Apply the **Entrance Fly In animation** and the **From Top-Left Effect Options** to the two bullets on Slide 6.

c. Apply the **Emphasis – Transparency animation** to the slide title on Slide 7 and set the timing to **After Previous** with a delay and duration of **01.00** second. Apply the **Entrance Fly In animation** to Figure 3.

d. Apply the **Wheel animation** to Figure 4 on Slide 8.

e. Apply the **Grow & Turn animation** to the table and the **Pulse animation** to the title placeholder on Slide 9. Change the order so that the title animation appears before the table animation.

Create a Web Presentation, Save and Close the Presentation

Your director would like to distribute a copy of the presentation outline and make the presentation available online for students who are not able to attend the presentation. Save and close the presentation.

a. Save the *02p_MotorcycleSafety_LastFirst* presentation.

b. Switch to Outline View. Modify the outline structure to display only Heading 1 and print as instructed.

c. Save the presentation as a PowerPoint Show (*.ppsx).

d. Close the file and submit based on your instructor's directions.

Integrate Microsoft Office Software

Each program in the Microsoft Office suite has its strength and specialty. Microsoft Word is a word processor used to create documents, such as letters, flyers, and reports. Microsoft Excel is a spreadsheet application used for extensive calculations of data sets. Microsoft PowerPoint is a presentation program which allows users to create unique and professional-looking presentations with animations and transitions. Microsoft Access is a database management program that is perfect for storing and analyzing company data collected over several years. Often, employees will use some or all four programs together while working on a comprehensive project.

Tasks

In a business organization, employees and office managers may be responsible for integrating data and information using all the Microsoft Office 2013 applications. This could include the following:

- Create files, handouts, and reports for a business meeting.
- Copy, paste, export, and import data and information from one application to another application.
- Calculate descriptive statistics and apply mathematical functions in Excel.
- Create a chart in Excel and link it to a Word document or a PowerPoint slide.

Skills

In addition to basic integration skills, employees should be able to do the following:

- Maintain a database containing a variety of data and information.
- Merge data and information using Word, Excel, or Access.
- Determine which application to use when creating documents.
- Practice good file management techniques, which include file naming, storing, and backup procedures.

Capstone Exercises

Create a Table and Import Data from an Excel Worksheet

You are the assistant director of the Information Technology department of Healthy Living Motorcycles, Inc., and you are in charge of maintaining the company's database, which contains the Employees, Products, and Suppliers tables. You want to store the shareholders' information in the same database too, so you want to create a Shareholders table. Since you already have the shareholders' mailing information in an Excel workbook, you import the data into the Shareholders table.

a. Start Access. Open the *02i_HealthyLiving.accdb* database and save it as **02i_HealthyLiving_LastFirst**.

b. Import the data in the *02i_Shareholders.xlsx* Excel file into a newly created table. Use the column headings from the Excel file, and let Access add the primary key. Save and name the table as **Shareholders**.

c. Modify the field properties as follows if necessary:

Field Name	Data Type	Field Size	Comments
ID	AutoNumber	Long Integer	• This is the primary key, and it is automatically created by Access. • Caption = Shareholder ID. • Make sure that Indexed is set to Yes (No Duplicates).
S_FirstName	Short Text	30	Caption = S_First Name
S_LastName	Short Text	30	Caption = S_Last Name
S_StreetAddress	Short Text	30	Caption = S_Street Address
S_City	Short Text	35	
S_State	Short Text	2	
S_Zip	Short Text	25	
S_Phone	Short Text	20	

d. Use the Input Mask Wizard to create an input mask for zip code in the Shareholders table. Accept the underscore as the placeholder and store the data without the symbols in the mask.

e. Use the Input Mask Wizard to create an input mask for the phone number using the default Input Mask format for Phone Number. Accept the underscore as the placeholder and store the data without the symbols in the mask.

f. View the data in the Shareholders table in Datasheet view and adjust column widths so all data is visible.

g. Save and close the table.

Export Data to an Excel File

You want to write a letter to shareholders who reside in the state of Virginia. Before you write the letter, you create a query in Access to locate the Virginia shareholders, export the results of the query to an Excel file, and use the data file later to write your letter.

a. Create a query in Access to find all shareholders living in Virginia, and name it **VA Shareholders**. Use all the fields in the Shareholders table except ID. Sort the results based on shareholder's last name.

b. Use the Export feature on the External Data tab to export the VA Shareholders query to an Excel file.

c. Save the document in the same location as the Access database solution and name it **02i_VaShareholders_LastFirst**.

a. Do not save the export steps. Close Access.

Enter Formulas

Your executive assistant has collected enough financial information to create the income statement for the current year. You also want to project the income statement for the next five years.

a. Open *02i_IncomeStatement.xlsx* in Excel and save it as **02i_IncomeStatement_LastFirst**.

b. Enter the following formulas in the corresponding cells:
- [**cell B8**] Gross profit = Sales – Cost of goods sold
- [**cell B13**] Total operating expenses = Selling expenses + Administrative expenses
- [**cell B17**] Income before taxes = Operating income – Interest expense
- [**cell B20**] Net income after taxes = Income before taxes – Income tax expense
- [**cell B23**] Earnings per share = Net income after taxes / Total # of outstanding shares

c. Copy the above formulas from column B to the corresponding cells in columns C:G.

d. Use absolute references and the projected rates in A26:B33 to project the financial figures for Year 2016 in ranges **C6:C7, C11:C12, C15:C16, C18**, and **C22**.

e. Copy the cell contents in ranges C6:C7, C11:C12, C15:C16, C18, and C22 to the corresponding cells and ranges in columns D:G. Delete any unnecessary cell entries.

Format Worksheet

To give the worksheet a professional look, you apply a document theme, merge cells to display the company and worksheet headings, widen columns, format headings, and apply cell styles. To keep track of the changes, you add your name and the date at the bottom of the worksheet. You also insert a footer to provide information of the worksheet. Finally, you preview and make necessary changes to ensure that the whole worksheet is displayed on one page.

a. Rename the first sheet tab name to **Income Statement** and change the sheet tab color to **Red**.

b. Apply the **Wisp Theme** to the entire worksheet.

c. Merge, center, and apply **Heading 1 Cell Styles** to the **range A1:G1** and increase the font size to **18**. Select the **Dark Red, Accent 1, Darker 50% font color**. Apply the **Dark Red, Accent 1, Lighter 40% fill color**.

d. Merge, center, and apply **Heading 2 Cell Styles** to the range **A2:G2** and increase the font size to **16**. Select the **Dark Red, Accent 1, Darker 25% font color**. Apply the **Dark Red, Accent 1, Lighter 80% fill color**.

e. Merge, center, and apply **Heading 3 Cell Styles** to the range **A3:G3** and increase the font size to **14**. Select the **Dark Red, Accent 1, Darker 50% font color**. Apply the **Dark Red, Accent 1, Lighter 60% fill color**. Move *Projected Income for the Next 5 Years* to the next line. If necessary, adjust all row heights as needed so that all headings are visibly displayed.

f. Apply **Heading 4 Cell Styles** to range A6:A33. Apply **Wrap Text** to **cell B25**.

g. Apply the **Total Cell Styles** to ranges B8:G8 and B20:G20.

h. Format the following cell ranges as follows:
- B6:G20 with Accounting Number Format and no decimal places.
- B22:G22 with comma and no decimal place.
- B23:G23 with Accounting Number Format and 2 decimal places.

i. Adjust column widths to display all content in cells.

j. Use an appropriate date function in **cell A34** to display today's date in your worksheet. Use the **Short Date format**.

k. Create a footer with your first name and last name on the left side, the Sheet Name in the center, and File Name on the right side of the worksheet.

l. Change orientation to **Landscape**, margin to **Narrow**, and bottom margin to **.5"**. Preview the worksheet to ensure that the whole worksheet fits on one page.

Create an Excel Chart

You create a 3D column chart for the projected EPS of the next five years.

a. Insert an apostrophe before the year in **cell B5** to format the years as text. Use the fill handle to copy the series to C5:G5. Select the content in ranges C5:G5 and C23:G23 and insert a 3D Column chart that shows the projected EPS for the next five years.

b. Apply the **Style 3 Chart Styles** to the chart.

c. Change the chart title to **Projected EPS for 2016–2020**. Increase the chart title font size to **28**.

d. Move the chart to a new separate chart sheet (following the worksheet). Name the tab as **EPS Column Chart** and change the sheet tab color to **Yellow**.

e. Save the worksheet and close the workbook. Submit documents to your instructor as instructed.

Modify the Cover Letter and Newsletter

Your company periodically mails out newsletters to shareholders. Your assistant has written a draft of the cover letter and the current issue of the company's newsletter. You modify the letter and the educational newsletter to make them look more professional before sending them to shareholders later.

a. Open the *02i_Newsletter.docx* document and save it as **02i_Newsletter_LastFirst**.

b. Convert the words *Healthy Living Motorcycles, Inc.* at the top of the document into a WordArt. Use the **WordArt Fill – Gold, Accent 4, Soft Bevel style**, and **28 font size**. Resize the placeholder so that the text displays on one line. Center the WordArt across the top of the letter.

c. Make the following changes to the letter:
- Replace *Current Date* with a date field that will update automatically.
- Insert **Educational information for Shareholders** after Re:
- Replace *Student First Name and Last Name* below *Sincerely Yours* with your own name at the bottom of the letter.
- Replace Student_First Name and Last Name at Student@ hl.com in the second paragraph with your own name and email address.

d. Format the whole document as follows:
- Set margin to **Normal**, font type to **Times New Roman**, and paragraph alignment to **Justified**.
- Select the text starting from *Educational Information* near the bottom of the first page to the end of the document, and set the paragraph Spacing After to **6 pt**.
- Apply the **Organic Theme** to the whole document.
- Show All Markup and insert a **DRAFT** watermark as directed in the first comment.
- Review all comments in the document and delete them.

Create Sections, Apply Styles, Modify Styles, and Change Bullet Image

The document describes several major topics of financial matters, and each topic is further broken into subtopics. You create a section to separate the cover letter from the newsletter, and format the titles and headings in each section using existing styles. You then modify the heading styles to enhance the appearance of the document. You experiment with several themes and apply a theme that you like.

a. Insert a **Section Break (Next Page)** to the left of the words *Educational Information* near the bottom of the first page. Apply the **Title style** to the section heading *Educational Information*. Modify the Title style to use **Times New Roman**, **bold**, **Green, Accent 1, Darker 25%, 6 pt** before and **12 pt** after. Apply **Align center**.

b. Apply the **Heading 1 style** to the following text in the document:

- *Introduction*
- *Understanding Financial Statement*
- *Understanding Financial Ratios*
- *Summary*
- *References*

c. Apply **Heading 2** style to the following headings:

- *Balance Sheet*
- *Income Statement*
- *Statement of Cash Flows*
- *Liquidity Ratios*
- *Leverage*
- *Rates of Return*
- *Stock Market Ratios*

d. Modify the Heading 1 style to use **Times New Roman, 16-pt**, **bold, Orange, Accent 5, Darker 25%**. Adjust the paragraph spacing to **6 pt** before and **6 pt** after, alignment to **Centered**, and Line spacing to **Single**.

e. Modify the Heading 2 style to use **Times New Roman, 14-pt**, **bold, Orange, Accent 5, Darker 25%**. Adjust the paragraph spacing to **0 pt** before and **6 pt** after, and Line spacing to **Single**.

f. Search the Internet for an image using the word *motorcycle*. Replace all the bullet lists with the downloaded motorcycle.

Insert a Worksheet from Excel

You want to show an example of an income statement in the newsletter. Because the income statement from the workbook is too large to show in portrait layout, you decide to insert two separate sections so that the income statement display on a landscape page.

a. Insert two Section Breaks (Next Page) on the blank line above the *Understanding Financial Ratios* heading.

b. Change the layout of the blank page to **Landscape**.

c. Open the *02i_IncomeStatement_LastFirst.xlsx* file using Excel. Select the worksheet **range A1:G23** from the Income Statement tab and copy and paste it to the landscape page. Adjust the column widths, if necessary, so that all the figures display on the same line. Ensure that the whole income statement displays on one page. Right-align all the currency figures.

d. Insert and center a figure caption below the chart. Add the caption title as **Example of an Income Statement**. Change the font type and size to **Times New Roman, 11 pt**, and adjust the paragraph spacing Before and After to **6 pt**.

Insert Table of Contents

You create a table of contents for the newsletter so that readers can navigate to the specific topic more quickly. To conserve paper, you decide to insert the table of contents on the blank line above *Sincerely yours* on the cover letter.

a. Position the inserting point on the blank line above *Sincerely yours* on the cover letter.

b. Click the **Table of Contents arrow** in the References tab and insert a Table of Contents with the **Automatic Table 1** format.

c. Change the font for the table of contents to **Times New Roman, 10 pt** and delete the word *Contents*. Delete the blank line above *Sincerely yours* so that the cover letter is on one page.

d. Save the document.

Insert a Footnote, Footer, and Hyperlinks

You insert a footnote on the first page of the newsletter to inform your reader that the sources are listed in the References section. You also insert the hyperlinks in the References section of the newsletter.

a. Insert the following footnote at the end of the first sentence in the Introduction section on page 2: **The materials in this newsletter are summarized from the sources listed in the References section of this document.**

b. Apply **Times New Roman, 11 pt** font to the footnote.

c. Position your cursor on page 1, insert the **Integral style** footer, and check the **Different First Page** box. Format the page number to start at **0**. Change the font type and size to **Times New Roman, 11 pt**.

d. Go to the References section on the last page of the newsletter, format the six sources as bullets, and **insert hyperlinks** to the six URLs.

Complete a Mail Merge

You conduct a mail merge to prepare a mailing to the shareholders residing in Virginia by merging the newsletter you have prepared with a data source that you had created using Access.

a. Move to the beginning of the document. Begin a new mail merge, creating letters using the current document. The data source is the *02i_VaShareholders_LastFirst.xlsx* Excel file.

b. You want to send the letters to only two recipients with the Lastnames of **Jones** and **Williams**.

c. Replace [Address Block] with the <<Address block>> field. Replace [first name] in salutation with the <<S_FirstName>>.

d. Merge all records, resulting in a seven-page document, with the cover letter and the newsletter addressed to only two Virginian shareholders. Note: If you are not using the Wizard, click Edit Recipient list to select the desired recipients.

e. Save the new document as **02i_MergedLetter_LastFirst** and close all documents.

Create the PowerPoint Slide Show

You will use the EPS Column chart that you created as part of a presentation to the shareholders by the finance department. You begin by creating a blank presentation and import an outline that your assistant had created for you. You then set up the title page, insert a header and footer, and apply a design and color theme to the document.

a. Open a blank PowerPoint slide show and save it as **02i_Finance_LastFirst.pptx**.

b. Enter the following text into the placeholders on the title slide:

- Title placeholder: **Healthy Living Motorcycles, Inc**. Change the font size to **55**.

- Subtitle placeholder: **Presented By: Student First Name Last Name.**

c. Search online and insert the clip art image of your choice using *motorcycle* as your keyword.

d. Change the height of the clip art image to **2"**.

e. Use the **Gradient Fill – Olive Green, Accent 4, Outline – Accent 4 WordArt** to add the company's initials (HLM) and put it on the right side of the image. [You may use any other WordArt of your choosing.] Group the WordArt and clip art to create a logo. Make other changes as desired, but do not exceed the 2" height requirement. Position the logo in the top-left quadrant of the title slide.

f. Create a slide footer that displays the current date, the slide number, and your First Name Last Name on each slide, except the title slide.

g. Create a handout header with your full name and a handout footer with your instructor's full name and the course number and title. Include the page number and the current date to update automatically.

h. Create Slide 2 using the Title and Content layout, and add **Agenda** as the slide title.

i. Insert another slide using the Title Only layout and insert **Any Questions?** as the title. Drag the placeholder to the middle of the page and center the title.

j. Apply the **Wisp theme**.

Import an Outline, Format the Slides, and Insert a Chart

You import the Word outline into the current presentation between the *Agenda* and *Any Questions* slides. You proceed to format the other slides and make them attractive.

a. Select the Agenda slide and import the *02i_Outline_LastFirst.rtf* outline file into the presentation.

b. Apply the format of the slide footer, handout header, and handout footer that you had created for Slide 2 to the newly added slides (3–9).

c. Open the *02i_IncomeStatement_LastFirst.xlsx* Excel file. Select the worksheet **range A1:G23** from the Income Statement tab

and copy and paste it to the right side of Slide 3. Apply the **Medium Style 2 - Accent 1 Table Style**, an outside border, and the **Brown Text 2, Lighter 60% Shading** option to the image. Increase the table height to **5"** and table width to **6.7"**.

d. Insert a new slide with the Title and Content layout after Slide 8. Copy and paste the EPS Column chart to Slide 9. Insert the slide title as **Comparison of EPS over Five Years**.

e. Resize the chart to a height of **4.4"**, and position it in the middle of the slide.

f. Populate the Agenda page with the titles of all the slides.

Add Animation

Now that the presentation has been created, add animations to introduce elements at appropriate times and to create visual interest.

a. Apply the **Wipe transition** to the page on Slide 1 and add the **Emphasis – Spin Effect** to the company logo.

b. Apply the **Split transition** on Slide 2 and set the timing to After.

c. Apply the **Shape animation** to the slide title on Slide 4, and set the timing to **After Previous** with a delay of **01.00** second. Apply the **Fly In animation** to the bullet list on this slide. Change the order so that the title appears after the bullets fly in.

d. Apply a **Fly In animation** to the chart, animating By Category on Slide 9.

e. Apply the **Grow & Turn animation** to the bullet list and the **Swivel animation** to the slide title on Slide 10. Change the order so that the title animation appears after the bullet list animation.

Create a Web Presentation, Save and Close the Presentation

You want to distribute a copy of the presentation outline to your audience and to make the presentation available online for anyone who is unable to attend the presentation. Save and close the presentation.

a. Run the slide show. Save the presentation.

b. Switch to Outline view. Modify the outline structure to display only Heading 1 and print as instructed.

c. Save the presentation as a PowerPoint Show (*.ppsx).

d. Close the file and submit all the documents to your instructor as instructed.

Education Discipline

Using Microsoft Office as an Educator

BACKGROUND | Teaching in a School System

Our educational system consists of many professionals and many levels of education. One can work in a private or public grade schools, middle schools, high schools, trade schools, colleges, and universities. Within each level of education there are a variety of positions. These include administrators such as superintendents, principals, deans, vice-presidents, chief financial officers; support professionals including curriculum specialists, librarians, school nurse, technology specialist; and educators.

For this capstone exercise, you will be assuming the role of a middle school (8th grade) teacher. The job of the teacher requires preparing lessons, presenting materials to students, enhancing their education with field trips and projects, calculating grades, maintaining records as required by the school district and various accrediting bodies, working with parents, staff, and other colleagues, and attending and presenting at conferences.

Teachers work with word processing, spreadsheets, databases, and presentation programs. You will be working with Microsoft Office to gain proficiency in using applications to create some of the necessary materials in your role as an 8th grade teacher.

Discipline Specific Capstones

Using Office in Education

Application	Exercises	Skills Covered
1. WORD Data Files: 03w_SchoolSupplies 03w_Rules 03w_School.jpg 03w_WashingtonMonument.jpg 03w_NewsletterImport1 03w_NewsletterImport2 03w_NewsletterImport3 03w_NewsletterImport4 03w_NewsletterImport5 03w_LessonImport Solution Files: 03w_SchoolSupplies_Solution 03w_Rules_Solution 03w_Rules_Solution.pdf 03w_RulesPoster_Solution 03w_Newsletter_Solution 03w_LessonTemp_Solution.dotx	Insert Title (page 49)	• Use a template • Check spelling and grammar • Insert headers and footers • Insert a symbol • Apply font attributes • Select paragraph alignment • Use indents and tabs • Create bullets • Work with sections • Apply styles • Insert objects into a document • Create and edit a table layout • Format a table • Use borders and shading • Create a source and include citation • Create a bibliography • Create and modify a footnote • Add and reply to comments
2. EXCEL Data Files: 03e_GradeBookImport 03e_GradeBookImport2 03e_BudgetDC2014 Solution Files: 03w_GradeBook_Solution 03e_BudgetDC2014_Solution	Insert Title (page 53)	• Create formulas • Use AutoFill • Manage the workbook and worksheets • Insert and delete cells, columns, and rows • Adjust column and row width and height • Hide and unhide columns • Work with ranges • Move, copy, and paste data • Apply number formats • Use page setup options • Use relative, absolute, and mixed cell references • Use the SUM function • Insert statistical functions • Insert the TODAY function • Use the IF function • Use the VLOOKUP function • Select the data source • Choose the chart type • Move a chart • Create a column chart • Create a pie chart • Format chart elements • Create sparklines • Freeze rows and columns • Set a print area • Create a table • Apply a table style • Sort data • Filter data • Use a total row
3. ACCESS Data Files: 03a_ReadingList 03a_GuardianInput.xlsx 03a_StudentInput.xlsx 03a_StudentGuardianInput.xlsx Solution Files: 03a_ReadlingList_Solution 03a_Student_Solution	Insert Title (page 57)	• Navigate among the objects in an Access database • Save as, compact and repair, and back up Access files • Sort data • Filter data • Use the Relationships window • Create a database using a template • Design a table • Create and modify tables • Work with multiple-table databases • Create a single-table query • Specify query criteria • Run a query • Create a multi-table query • Modify a multi-table query • Create a calculated field in a query • Create expressions with the Expression Builder • Use built-in functions in Access • Add aggregate functions to the datasheets • Create queries with aggregate functions • Create forms using the form tools • Work with form layout control • Sort records in a form • Create reports using the report tools • Modify a report • Sort records in a report

| 4. POWERPOINT
Data Files: 03p_Rules.docx
03p_Principal.jpg
03p_Smith.jpg
03p_Alison.jpg
03p_Wagoner.jpg
03p_Klosky.jpg
03p_Computer.jpg
03p_Librarian.jpg
03p_DCSkyline.jpg
03p_speakernotesrules.docx

Solution Files:
03p_OrientCR_Solution | Insert Title
(page 61) | • Plan and create a presentation • Insert media objects and tables • Use animations and transitions • Insert headers and footers • Run and navigate a slide show • Print notes page and handouts • Create a presentation using a template • Modify a template • Reuse slides from an existing presentation • Modify a slide master • Create shapes • Create SmartArt • Create WordArt • Modify objects • Arrange objects • Insert a picture • Transform a picture • Use the Internet as a resource |
| 5. INTEGRATED
Data Files:
03i_PermissionLetter.docx
03i_Students.accdb
03i_OctoberNewsletter.docx
03i_BudgetDC2014Updated.xlsx
03i_ReadingBooks.jpg
03i_LessonPlanOriginal.docx
03i_LessonPlanOriginal_MS.docx
03i_ParentOpenHouse.pptx
03i_POrientation.pptx

Solution Files:
03i_PermissionLetter_Solution.docx
03i_Students_Solution.accdb
03i_MergedPermissionLetter_Solution.docx
03i_OctoberNewsletter_Solution.docx
03i_BudgetDC2014Updated_Solution.xlsx
03i_LessonPlanOriginal_Solution.docx
03i_LessonPlanFinal_Solution.docx
03i_ParentOpenHouse_Solution.pptx | Insert Title
(page 65) | • Create a primary document in Word and use Access as the data source file • Import data from Access into Excel to create the grading workbook • Embed and link content from multiple sources into a newsletter • Embed content from Excel into a PowerPoint presentation • Use track changes to revise the lesson plan template • Share the lesson plan with other teachers via OneDrive |

Use Microsoft Word

Background

Teachers are responsible for a variety of tasks. Among these tasks are preparing and presenting instructional materials; managing the educational environment (student conduct); record-keeping tasks such as grades and attendance records; ordering supplies; communicating with students, parents, and peers; presenting subject matter; assessing student learning; and pursuing professional development. Word processing skills are critical for accomplishing some of these tasks in an efficient, effective manner.

Tasks

In a smaller school district, the teacher may be responsible for a variety of documents, including the following:

- Lesson plans
- Parent newsletter
- Classroom flyer
- Grading rubric

In a larger school district, where the instructional and technology staff develop tools to assist the teacher and to ensure compliance with standards, the teacher may still be responsible for the following:

- Complete and adjust templates as necessary
- Use predesigned daily planners
- Prepare documents for posting to the school or teacher Web site

Skills

In addition to opening a document, saving it, and basic formatting, a teacher should be able to do the following:

Chapter 1

- Use a template
- Check spelling and grammar
- Insert headers and footers
- Insert a symbol

Chapter 2

- Apply font attributes
- Select paragraph alignment
- Use indents and tabs
- Create bullets
- Work with sections
- Apply styles
- Insert objects into a document

Chapter 3

- Create and edit a table layout
- Format a table
- Use borders and shading

Chapter 4

- Create a source and include citation
- Create a bibliography
- Create and modify a footnote
- Add and reply to comments

EDUCATORS

Capstone Exercises

You are preparing for the start of the school year. This requires you to create several documents, which will save you time as you prepare for the school year. You will also need to create some orientation materials such as a supplies checklist, a flyer and poster with classroom rules, a welcome newsletter for the parents, and a sample grading rubric. You will also need to develop a lesson plan template that you will use to create your unit or weekly lessons and a daily planner to keep yourself on track.

Create a New Document and Select a Style

The policy of the school district is to have the students purchase their own supplies. As the teacher, you are responsible for creating a list of supplies required for the school year. You will open a document with a list of supplies, rename it, and then add and format a title. This document will list supplies required for 8th grade students.

a. Open *03w_SchoolSupplies* and rename the file as **03w_SchoolSupplies_LastFirst**.

b. Type **School Supplies List** at the top of the page and press **Enter** two times.

c. Format *School Supplies List* as **Title** style. **Center** the title.

Add a Header, Adjust Line Spacing, Set Tabs, and Insert a Symbol

This school supply list was generated during a planning session with the other 8th grade teachers, but each of you are responsible for adjusting the list for your students. You will add a header with your name and grade level, adjust line spacing, insert a rectangular bullet in front of each item, adjust the tab setting, and then add a signature line. The form will be signed by the parent or guardian and returned to you when all supplies are purchased.

a. Insert a Header using **Blank** style. Display the Ruler if necessary.

b. Type **Mrs. Smith** at the left margin. Remove the **Center** Tab from the Ruler.

c. Type **8th Grade** at the *Right Tab* mark. Close the Header.

d. Set the line spacing for the list of items to **Double**. Set *Spacing After* to **0 pt**.

e. Apply **Bullets** to the list of items to purchase. Change the Bullet style to an **empty rectangle bullet** symbol. Students can then check off the items purchased so they can see what is left to buy.

f. Go to the end of the document and insert 2 blank lines. Remove the bullets.

g. On the second or last blank line, set the indent to 3" on the horizontal ruler. Type Parent or Guardian Signature. Set a Right Tab at the 6.5" mark. Press Tab and type Date.

h. Insert a shape line about 1/4" above the text just typed extending from the 3" mark to the 6.5" mark.

i. **Save** the document and close it.

Modify a Document

You want to go over the classroom rules and discuss them with your students. You decide to create a flyer for each student and post that information on the four walls of the classroom.

a. Open *03w_Rules* and save it as **03w_Rules_LastFirst**.

b. Run the **Spelling & Grammar** checker. Make the corrections as appropriate.

c. Adjust the font size of all the text in the list to **20 pt**. Change the first letter of the first rule to **36 pt, Bold**. Change the first letter of the rest of the rules to **36 pt, Bold**, using the **Format Painter**.

d. Change the color of every other first letter to **red** starting with the first rule.

e. Insert a page border using the **people art** work, set the width to **20 pt**, and then use **Standard Red**. The people art work looks like Figure 3.1.

f. Select all text and create a hanging indent at the **1/4"** mark.

g. Insert an online picture from **Office.com Clip Art** at the top of the document on a blank line. Search the selection using the phrase **classroom full of students raising their hands**.

h. Adjust the size of the clip art so the width is **2"** and the height is **1.12"**, removing the *Lock aspect ratio* check mark. You want to keep this flyer to one page.

i. Insert WordArt to the right of the clip art image, selecting **Fill, Red - Accent 2, Outline - Accent 2**.

j. Type **Classroom Rules**. Move the WordArt so the right edge of the WordArt placeholder is at the **6"** horizontal ruler mark. Drag the left side of the WordArt placeholder to the right edge of the clip art. Apply Text Effect **Bevel, Circle** to the WordArt. Apply Text Fill **Standard Red** to the WordArt.

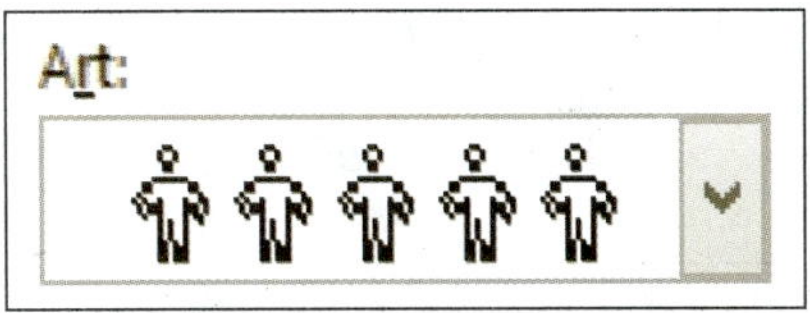

FIGURE 3.1 PEOPLE ART PAGE BORDER

k. **Save** the document. Now resave it as a **PDF file** so the IT department can upload it to the school's Web site. Close the PDF file.

Change the Formatting

Next you want to use the flyer you created to make a poster for displaying in the classroom. You will need to adjust the paper and font size.

a. Open the *03w_Rules_LastFirst.docx* file, if necessary. Change the paper size to **Legal Paper.**

b. Select all the text rules and change the font to **36 pt**. Select the first letter of each rule and change the font size to **48 pt**.

c. Adjust line spacing of the rules to **Single, 6 pt After**.

d. Adjust the font size of the WordArt to **48 pt** and adjust the positioning of the WordArt so it is centered between the clip art and paper border. Adjust the right side of the WordArt placeholder so the text fits on one line. Note this poster should fit on one page.

e. Save the document as **03w_RulesPoster_LastFirst**. Close the document.

Use a Template

You now want to create the first newsletter for this academic year. You will use a template so you don't have to spend time with the formatting. You will replace that content with your content.

a. Open a new document using *School Newsletter* as the search term in the *Search for online templates* search box. Select the *Elementary school newsletter* template and save the file as **03w_Newsletter_LastFirst**.

b. Replace the following text:
Month: **August**
Organization: **Fort Pitt Middle School**

c. Replace the [*Street, City, ST ZIP Code*], [*Website*], and [*Telephone*] with **401 William St., Pittsburgh, PA 15213; https:// www.fortpitt.K12.pa.us/fortpitt**; and **999-000-1111**, respectively. This means to click the bracket [] with the text and type the replacement text.

d. Insert the picture **03w_School.jpg** on the first page replacing the current picture.

e. Replace the text starting *Dear Reader* through Word with the text in *03w_NewsletterImport1*. If you have an extra line after Klosky, delete it.

f. Replace the text *Make It Your Own through newsletter* with the text in the file *03w_NewsletterImport2*.

g. Adjust the text, if necessary, on the first page of the newsletter by deleting extra paragraph marks or line spacing to make it fit on the first page. Check the second page to make sure the text doesn't run onto it.

h. Select the following dates of the current year from the drop-down calendar and type the following events in the Upcoming Events section on the first page:
September 13   **Fall Festival**
October 18   **Homecoming**
October 26   **Pumpkin Social**

i. Replace using copy and paste the content in the Important Announcement section with the text in the file *03w_NewsletterImport3*. Make sure there are appropriate paragraph breaks when the text is pasted into the newsletter.

j. Import the text in the file *03w_NewsletterImport4* to the second page below *More Important News*.

k. Replace the picture on page 2 with **03w_WashingtonMonument. jpg**.

l. Replace the text below *In the Community* with the text in *03w_NewsletterImport5*. Adjust the text, if necessary, to make sure there is a blank space between paragraphs.

m. **Save** and close the file.

Create a Template

You now want to create a template to use when developing your lesson plans. Each unit of content requires a lesson plan that meets the requirements set forth by the district. You will create a section break, alter the page orientation, and then insert and format a table. You will also add a footnote.

Use a Section Break, Adjust Page Orientation, and Insert a Table

a. Open the document *03w_LessonImport* and save the file as a template, naming it **03w_LessonTemp_LastFirst.dotx**.

b. Go to the end of the document and insert a **Section Break, Next Page**. Set the page orientation to **Landscape** for page 2.

c. Insert a **5×3 table** on page 2.

d. Type the following in the table as shown below. Make sure you format the text in the second row as **Italics**.

Content Outline	Instructional Methods	Procedures	Materials	Evaluation/ Assessment
[Place the general outline of content here.]	*[What will the teacher do? What will the learner do? Examples include discussions, projects, lectures, demonstrations, exercises, and so forth]*	*[Provide a step-by-step list of what will be done.]*	*[List materials needed. For example, computer with Internet connection, poster board and notecards.]*	*[How will you assess learner's achievement of objectives?]*

e. Format the table *Header* row with a **double borderline** on all four sides. Apply the Theme Color, **White Background 1, Darker 15% shading** to the Header row.

f. Insert the following footnote after Information Literacy in the Academic Standard line near the top of page 1.

You may substitute the appropriate standard here. The example standard can be found at http://www.iste.org/docs/ pdfs/nets-s-standards.pdf?sfvrsn=2

g. Save and submit based on instructors' direction. Note: Some instructors may require you to create a folder, place the five files in the folder, zip (compress) the folder, and then send the zipped folder to them. Close the document and Word.

Use Microsoft Excel

Background

Microsoft Excel permits the teacher to organize numbers and display results of calculations, and thereby make his or her job more efficient and effective. Even when school districts provide online grade access for generating grade reports, in many cases the teacher must complete the calculations and upload the grades. The teacher should look at Excel as a way to streamline any and all number management tasks as well as statistical calculations that may be necessary for meeting required standards. In addition, teachers must also deal with some budgetary issues related to the classroom and other extracurricular activities.

Tasks

The teacher may be responsible for worksheet tasks such as:
- Calculating grades.
- Preparing charts of assessment progress.
- Preparing classroom budgets.
- Submitting travel expenses for meetings and conferences.

Skills

In addition to opening, saving, printing, and basic formatting skills, a teacher should be able to do the following:

Chapter 1

- Create formulas
- Use AutoFill
- Manage the workbook and worksheets
- Insert and delete cells, columns, and rows
- Adjust column and row width and height
- Hide and unhide columns

- Work with ranges
- Move, copy, and paste data
- Apply number formats
- Use page setup options

Chapter 2

- Use relative, absolute, and mixed cell references
- Use the SUM function
- Insert statistical functions
- Insert the TODAY function
- Use the IF function
- Use the VLOOKUP function

Chapter 3

- Select the data source
- Choose the chart type
- Move a chart
- Create a column chart
- Create a pie chart
- Format chart elements
- Create sparklines

Chapter 4

- Freeze rows and columns
- Set a print area
- Create a table
- Apply a table style
- Sort data
- Filter data
- Use a total row

Capstone Exercises

As a teacher in this school system, you will need to develop two spreadsheets to calculate and record student grades and to manage the scheduled field trip budget. You will need to set up a grading sheet for each of your classes that will calculate letter grades after you enter the raw scores for all the student graded activities. The field trip will require a budget outlining the costs, what is actually in the account, and what is left to be raised.

Create a New Workbook, Add Labels, and Rename the Worksheet (Grade Book)

You will create a new blank worksheet, add labels to it, rename the worksheet, and save the worksheet. This worksheet will contain the grades for grading period 1 for the English class taught during class period 1.

a. Open a *new blank workbook* and rename it **03e_GradeBook_LastFirst**.

b. In **cell A1** type **Academic Year 2014-2015** (you may substitute the current academic year here).

c. In **cell A2** type **Virginia Smith** and in **cell A3 8th Grade English Class Period 1**.

d. Type the following labels in the corresponding cells:
   B5   **Grading Period 1**
   A6   **Name**
   B6   **Assign1** and AutoFill this label through I6 so it ends with Assign8
   J6   **Total Points**
   K6   **Percentage**
   L6   **Letter Grade**

e. Rename *Sheet 1* to **GradingPeriod1**. Add 1 new Sheet. Rename the new sheet **RangeName**.

Use the SUM, TODAY, and LOOKUP Functions, Insert a Row, and Create a Range Name

You are ready now to continue setting up the worksheet by inserting a function to sum the grades for the first grading period and look up their letter equivalent. You realize you should date this worksheet to display the current date on this worksheet. You believe this belongs somewhere under the worksheet identifying information, which will require you to insert a new row.

a. In the *GradingPeriod1* worksheet, enter a function in **cell J7** that adds assignments for Grading Period 1 (assignments 1–8).

b. Insert a **row** between rows 4 and 5.

c. Insert a function in **cell A4** that displays the current date when you open the workbook.

d. In *G6*, type **Total Possible Points** and in *J6*, **400**. In *K8*, calculate a percentage grade for each student based on student

earned points (J column) based on the total possible points in **J6**. Format K8:K27 as **percentage**.

e. Go to the *RangeName* worksheet. In **cell A1** type **Grades**. Select the range **A2:B7**. Now enter the data below, pressing the enter key after each item but the last one.

Percentage	Letter Grade
0%	F
60%	D
70%	C
80%	B
90%	A

f. Create a range name called **Grades** for the range A3:B7.

g. In the GradingPeriod1 worksheet, insert a function in **cell L8** that will return a letter grade in column L based on the percent score in column K.

Copy the Formulas and Enter Data

First, you will need to copy the two formulas down the rows and enter some sample data to test that your worksheet functions perform as intended before you enter actual student data. You will then need to make changes if errors are noted. These data will then be deleted and student data entered.

a. Copy the formulas in the range *J8:L8* through **J9:L11**.

b. In **cell A8** type **Student 1** and use AutoFill through **A11**. In **cell B8** type **50**, in **cell B9 30**, in cell **B10 41**, and in cell **B11 1**. Use AutoFill to copy the values in *B8:B11* through column **I**.

c. Check to make sure the results in columns J and K are correct, that the correct letter grade has been assigned based on the total points earned converted to a percentage. If not, check your formulas for any errors. For example, did you make a typo for the range name or forget to apply the range name to the workbook when you created it?

d. Delete the data in range A8:I11 to remove the sample data now that the formulas have been tested. Do not delete the formulas or the headings.

e. Save the workbook.

Format the Worksheet, Add and Sort the Student Data, and Prepare to Print

Now that you have the worksheet designed, you will need to copy the student data into the worksheet, finalize the worksheet by improving its appearance, and place the students' names in alphabetical order for easier use.

a. Open *03e_GradeBookImport*. Copy the data from this workbook into the GradePeriod1 worksheet of the

03e_GradeBook_LastFirst with the student data in range **A8:I27**. Close the 03e_GradeBookImport workbook.

b. Copy the formulas in *J8:L8* through *J27:L27*.

c. Format the cell contents in rows *1:7* as **Bold**. Change the font of the text in A1 to **16 pt**.

d. Merge and center **A1:L1**, **A2:L2**, and **A3:L3**. Apply the **Yellow** Fill Color to B6:L6.

e. Wrap the text in **cell J7** and **L7**. Adjust the **column widths** so all data are visible with J7 and L7 showing the text on two lines. Place **All Borders** around the cells in range *A8:L27*. **Align Right cell J7**.

f. Sort the student data in alphabetic order from A to Z by name.

g. Create a Footer with your name in the center and the Sheet Name code in the right area. Exit the footer. Set the worksheet to print in Landscape. Save the file.

Use Statistical Functions

The school district now requires that some statistical functions like highest score, lowest score, and average score be available for all assignments and the distribution of letter grades for each grading period.

a. Make sure the 03e_GradeBook_LastFirst is open and you are on the GradingPeriod1 worksheet.

b. Type **Assignment Statistics** in cell **A29**, **Bold** the text in A29, set the Font to **12 pt**, and **Merge & Center** cells A29:L29.

c. Copy the labels for all the assignments (B7:I7) to B30:I30. Do not include the Total, Percentage, or Letter Grade columns.

d. Type **Lowest Score** in A31, **Highest Score** in A32, and **Average Score** in A33.

e. Enter a function in **cell B31** to calculate the lowest score for Assign1. Enter a function in B32 to calculate the highest score for Assign1. Enter a function in B33 to calculate the average score for Assign1. Copy all three functions through Assign8 (range C31:I33).

f. In **cell A35** type **Grading Period 1 Letter Grade Distribution**. **Bold** and **Merge & Center** across range A35:L35. If necessary, change the font to **12 pt**.

g. In **cell E36** type **A**, in **E37** type **B**, in **E38** type **C**, in **E39** type **D**, and in **E40** type **F**.

h. In **cell F36**, include a function to count the number of As. AutoFill the function in F37, F38, F39, and F40, checking for Bs, Cs, Ds, and Fs, respectively. Use the COUNTIF(range of cells to count, "Letter Value"). Make sure the range of cells is absolute. Once copied, change the letter grade to the appropriate one ie B, C, and so forth.

i. Adjust the worksheet to **Fit Sheet On One Page** for printing purposes.

Copy a Worksheet and Delete Data

As the first grading period ends, you will need to create the second grading period.

a. Copy the *GradingPeriod1* worksheet creating a new worksheet. Name the new worksheet **GradingPeriod2**. Delete all the data in **cells B8:I27** on the *GradingPeriod2* worksheet.

b. Check for accuracy in the letter grade count as they should all be counted as F's. The average calculation will also show an error message since it is dividing by 0. This will be corrected once Grading Period 2 data are entered.

c. In **cells B6** and **A35**, change the Grading Period from 1 to 2. Change the fill color of the Grading Period 2 range B6:L6 from yellow to Standard Color; Light Green. Change the GradingPeriod2 Tab Color to Light Green. Change the GradingPeriod1 Tab Color to Yellow.

d. Open *03e_GradeBookImport2* and copy the data in range **B1:D20** into range **B8:D27** on GradingPeriod2 worksheet.

e. Save the workbook.

Insert Pie, Column, and Sparkline Charts

The principal requests a chart so he can "see" the statistical results. You will first create a pie chart of the letter grade distribution and a column chart of Assignment 3.

a. Make sure the *03e_GradeBook_LastFirst* workbook is open and the *GradingPeriod1* worksheet is active.

b. Create a **3D pie** chart that shows the letter grade distribution for Grading Period 1. Place the chart at range H36:N46 on the GradingPeriod1 worksheet.

c. Create a chart title called **Grading Period 1 Letter Grade Distribution**. **Bold** the title. Change the font size of the title to 14pts.

d. Display More Data Labels Option and format the Data Labels with **Category Name**, **Percentage**, and **Leader Lines** showing. Remove the **Value Label** and the **Legend**. Place the data labels on the **Outside End**. Move the data labels out so that the leader line shows.

e. Change the Pie color option to **Colorful, Color 4**.

f. Create a **3D Clustered Column** chart of Assignment 3 that includes the Assignment 3 scores for each student. Place this chart on its own worksheet and name the worksheet **GP1-Assign3**. Move **GP1-Assign3** between the GradingPeriod1 and RangeName worksheets. Change the Sheet Tab Color to **Yellow**.

g. On the 3D column chart, create a primary vertical axis title called **Raw Scores** and a primary horizontal axis title called **Students**. Title the chart **Assignment 3 Results**. **Bold** the chart Title.

h. On the GradingPeriod1 worksheet, type **Grade Trend** in **cell M7**. **Wrap the Text** in **cell M7** and set the font size to **12 pt**. In **cell M8**, insert a **Column Sparkline** that shows all assignment scores for Paul Abba. Copy this chart through M27. Save the file.

Enlarge and Adjust a Chart

You decide that the charts are too small to read so you want to enlarge them and adjust the print size.

a. Enlarge the pie chart so it spans range **I36:R49** on the GradingPeriod1 worksheet.

b. Set the data label font size to **12 pt, Bold**. Use the 3D Rotation to set the X rotation to **30 degrees**.

Create a Table, Format the Table, and Filter Data

Sometimes teachers are ask to provide a list of students meeting certain criteria, for example a list of students with As or Fs on certain assignments or who might qualify for certain academic competitions. You will first create a table and filter that table by certain criteria. In this case, you are looking for students who had 45 or better on the first three assignments to provide that list to the principal. You will need to print the filtered data.

a. Make sure *03e_GradeBook_LastFirst* is open. Copy the GradingPeriod1 worksheet to a new worksheet called **TableGP1**. Move the TableGP1 worksheet between GradingPeriod1 and GP1-Assign3.

b. On the TableGP1 worksheet, create a table using range **A7:L27**. Apply filters to the Grading Period 1 table to show only students who have **45 or greater** on the first three assignments.

c. Set the print area to include the column headings for the first three assignments and the three students and their scores on the first three assignments.

d. Save the workbook.

Add an IF Function

You decide you want to include a note to students who did well this grading period. You want to do this for students with A grades.

a. Go to the GradingPeriod1 worksheet. Type **Note** in **cell N7**. **Bold** it.

b. In **cell N8**, create an IF statement that sends the message *Great job this grading period* for all students with As and leaves the cell blank if the statement is false.

c. Save and close the workbook.

Create a Budget Workbook

The other workbook you need to create deals with the upcoming trip to Washington, D.C. You know it is important to keep track of costs and make sure the money is sufficient to cover the costs. The budget reflects what you know from previous years as well as some estimated costs from the bus company, hotel, and pizza/pool party.

a. Open *03e_BudgetDC2014* and save it as **03e_BudgetDC2014_LastFirst**.

b. Add your name in **cell A4** after Prepared by. Place a data function in **cell A5** that displays the current date.

c. Enter the following numbers that reflect money already in the account:

C9	8000
C10	4419
C13	500

d. In **cell C14**, sum C9:C13.

Enter a Formula and Format the Worksheet

The upcoming fall and pumpkin festivals are quickly approaching. You want to know how much money must be raised by these two activities to cover the projected costs. You also want to share this information with the principal and parents.

a. In **cell A25** type **Resources Needed**. Format the text as **Bold**, **12 pt**, **Align Right**.

b. In **cell B25**, enter a formula to calculate the total amount of money that needs to be raised by the remaining two fund raisers to reach the goal of $18,300.

c. Format the values in **B9:C9**, **B13:C13**, **B18:C18**, and **B22:C22** as **Accounting**, **no decimal points**. Format the numbers in between those rows as **comma**, **no decimal points**. Format the Total rows and Resources Needed as **Accounting**, **no decimal points**.

d. Insert the **Oval Callout** from the Illustrations, Shapes and point it to **cell B25**. Make it approximately **2" × 2"**. Change the color of the callout to **Red**.

e. In the callout, type **We will have to work hard at the remaining fundraisers to meet our costs.**

f. Save and submit based on instructors' direction. Close the worksheet and Excel.

Use Microsoft Access

Background

A database can support some of the teacher's required record keeping and housekeeping tasks via quick and easy report generation. While some larger school districts maintain larger database management systems using Oracle or specially designed programs like Orbund's NEWTON, Rediker's Administrator's Plus, or School Recordkeeper's School Recordkeeper K-12, many opportunities still exist for a teacher to make use of a Microsoft Access database for smaller, more individualized projects. In addition, the costs of the larger databases may be out of reach for teachers in smaller school systems. Access is a good tool for any task requiring management of data that the teacher must complete. Even if the school district does not use an Access database, learning about the structure and capabilities of a database will make the teacher more effective in using other database programs.

Tasks

Especially in smaller and rural school systems, the teacher may be responsible for using Access to prepare the following:

- Develop contact database of students
- Maintain a reading list of acceptable books for the reading program
- Create database of classroom resources

Skills

In addition to opening, saving, printing, and basic data entry skills, a teacher should be able to do the following:

Chapter 1

- Navigate among the objects in an Access database
- Save as, compact and repair, and back up Access files
- Sort data
- Filter data
- Use the Relationships window
- Create a database using a template

Chapter 2

- Design a table
- Create and modify tables
- Work with multiple-table databases
- Create a single-table query
- Specify query criteria
- Run a query
- Create a multi-table query
- Modify a multi-table query

Chapter 3

- Create a calculated field in a query
- Create expressions with the Expression Builder
- Use built-in functions in Access
- Add aggregate functions to the datasheets
- Create queries with aggregate functions

Chapter 4

- Create forms using the form tools
- Work with form layout control
- Sort records in a form
- Create reports using the report tools
- Modify a report
- Sort records in a report

EDUCATORS

Capstone Exercises

While the school district IT department is responsible for the main larger databases necessary to keep track of all the data mandated by the federal and state education agencies, as a teacher in a local school district you will be responsible for maintaining a contact list of your students in case of emergencies. You are also responsible for keeping track of supplies and other classroom resources, especially when lending them to students or needing to reorder supplies. You are also responsible for keeping track of books acceptable for the reading program so you can make recommendations to parents regarding appropriate books. This will require you to work with a database to enter data, create queries, and generate reports.

Create an Entry Form and Update and Sort a Table

The school district has an initiative to get students to read by providing selected lists of recommended books. Each student is to read two books from the list in the fall and spring semesters and three over the summer. As you prepare for the fall semester, you need to review the Reading List database to make changes and updates. You want to do this with a simple input form to make this easier.

a. Open *03a_ReadingList* database and save it as **03a_Reading-List_LastFirst**. If necessary, click the Enable Content button. Open the Booklist table.

b. Create a **form** using the Form Wizard to enter new books to the table. Place all fields in the form and use columnar layout. Name the form **BookList**.

c. Add the following records using the *BookList* form and save and close the form.
   Krakauer, Jon, Into The Wild, Anchor Books, 10, Medium, Fall
   Krakauer, Jon, Three Cups Of Deceit: How Greg Mortenson, Humanitarian Hero Lost His Way, Anchor Books, 10, Hard, Spring
   Krakauer, Jon, Where Men Win Glory: The Odyssey Of Pat Tillman, Anchor Books, 10, Medium, Summer
   Guterson, David, Snow Falling On Cedars, Harcourt Books, 10, Medium, Spring
   Green, John, The Fault In Our Stars, Dutton Books, 10, Easy, Summer

d. Open and sort the BookList table by author in ascending order. Save the table.

Query the Database and Generate a Report

You want to find all the books on the list that are at a 10th grade reading level to provide that list to a few parents and students. These students need to be challenged more as they are excellent readers.

a. With the database still open, create a query to display all the **10th grade level** books, displaying the LName, FName, Title, and GradeLevel fields.

b. Save the query as **10thGradeLevel**.

c. Create a **report** using the Report Wizard based on the *10thGradeLevel* query. Show the last and first name of the author and title but not the GradeLevel field. Accept the defaults but change the title of the report to **Books for Students at the 10th Grade Level**.

d. In Design View, expand the title placeholder to the left and right margins. **Center** and **Bold** the title text.

e. Staying in Design View, shrink the Last Name field to the 1.5" mark, move the First Name field between the 1.5-3" mark, and expand the Title between the 3-8" mark, thereby showing all of the title text. Make these adjustments for both the Page Header and Details sections of the report.

f. Save the report and close the database.

Create a Database

Many excellent templates are available in Access, but some of them are more complex than is needed for your task. For example, the Desktop Student Database template contains information about health insurance, health insurance numbers, physicians, and the physicians' phone numbers. You decide to create your own student database that will keep track of the students, their guardians, and their attendance record. You will start by creating a blank database that will hold the necessary tables, reports, and queries. You will first create the Guardian table.

a. Open Access and create a *Blank Desktop* database. Save the database as **03a_Student_LastFirst**.

b. Go to Design view. Name the Table **Guardian**. Create the following fields, data types, and field properties for the Guardian table. Save the table once you create the structure.

GuardianID	Data Type Number	Field Size Long Integer	Primary Key
PrimaryGuardian	Data Type Yes/No	Default Yes	Caption Primary Guardian
GuardianFirst	Data Type Short Text	Field Size 30	Caption Guardian First Name
GuardianLast	Data Type Short Text	Field Size 30	Caption Guardian Last Name
EmailAddress	Data Type Hyperlink	N/A	Caption Email Address
BPhone	Data Type Short Text	Input Mask Phone Number with symbols in mask. Field Size 14	Caption Business Phone Number
CPhone	Data Type Short Text	Input Mask Phone Number	Caption Cell Phone Number with symbols in mask. Field Size 14
Notes	Data Type Short Text	Field Size 255	

c. Enter a Test Record. Type your information into the table using your first and last name but fake data for phone numbers and notes fields. Make sure you enter 5000 for the GuardianID number. Save and close the table.

d. Import the *03a_GuardianInput.xlsx* Excel file to the *03a_Student_LastFirst* database, *Guardian Table*. Use the append records option.

e. Save and close the table.

Create the Student Table

The school IT department provided you with an Excel file that contains the needed student data for this database. You will now import this Excel file into a new student table so you can connect students with their guardians.

a. Import the *03a_StudentInput.xlsx* file, creating a new table using the following settings during the import process.

- Do not permit duplicates for the StudentID field.
- Change the data type of StudentID to Long Integer and the EmailAddress field data type to hyperlink.
- Select your own primary key (StudentID).

b. Save the table as **Student**.

Create the StudentGuardian Table

a. Import the Excel *03a_StudentGuardianInput.xlsx* file into a new table in the 03a_Student_LastFirst database using the following settings:

- Set GuardianID with no duplicates permitted.
- GuardianID and StudentID data type is long integer.
- Choose your own primary key.

b. Save the table as **StudentGuardian**.

Create and Enforce Relationships

Now that you have the three tables created you want to create relationships between them.

a. Close any open tables.

b. Open the *Relationships* window. Add the three tables to the Relationships window.

c. Create a relationship between the **StudentGuardian** table and the **Student** table using the **StudentID** field; enforce referential integrity.

d. Create a second relationship between the **Guardian** table and the **StudentGuardian** table using the **GuardianID**; enforce referential integrity.

e. Save and close the Relationships window.

Create a Multi-Table Query

Create a query that displays students with health issues, on medications, and the emergency contact person.

a. Create a query in Design view; include the **Student**, **Guardian**, and **StudentGuardian** tables.

b. Add the following fields from the *Student* table: **Lname**, **Fname**, **SpecialCondition**, and **Medication**. From the *Guardian* table select the **GuardianLast**, **GuardianFirst**, **PrimaryGuardian**, and CPhone fields.

c. In the criteria row show only records where special condition is **not blank** and primary is **Yes**.

d. Run the query.

e. Save the query as **StudentHealthIssues**. Close the query.

Copy and Modify a Query

Now that you have the basics of creating a query, you want to see how many students have either an allergy or are on medications as you plan for the field trip in November.

a. Copy the *StudentHealthIssues* query; paste the query and call it **StudentAllergyMeds**.

b. In Design View, delete the **SpecialCondition** field and add the **Allergies** field. Move the Allergies field to the right of student's first name.

c. Set the criteria for Medications **not blank** OR Allergies **not blank**.

d. Run the query. Filter the **PrimaryGuardian** field to show the student's primary guardian. Ten records are displayed.

e. Save and close the query.

Create the Attendance Table

The last table you need to create is the attendance table. State requirements mandate that attendance be taken for each class. You will create the table and enter some data for testing purposes.

a. In the *Student* database, create an **Attendance** table with the following fields.

StudentID	Data Type Number	Field Size **Long Integer**
AttendDate	Data Type Date/Time	
Attendance	Data type **Short Text**	Field Size **15** Lookup combo box **Present, Absent-Excused, Absent-Unexcused**

Remove the primary key from the StudentID field.

b. Add the following data to the **Attendance** table.

StudentID	8001	AttendDate	8/25/2014	Attendance	Present
StudentID	8002	AttendDate	8/25/2014	Attendance	Absent-Excused

c. Save and close the table. Import *03a_AttendanceInput* Excel file and append the data to the **Attendance** table.

d. Open the **Relationship** window, add the Attendance table to the right of the Student table, and then establish a relationship between the Students and Attendance tables based on **StudentID**. Save and close the Relationships tab.

Create a Query for Missed Days for Students Absent from School

The school district has a policy about how many absent days a student can have before a letter is triggered to the guardian. You want to first test your table and query results to make sure there are no errors.

a. Create a query using the **Attendance** and **Student** tables.

b. Add the following fields: **StudentID**, **AttendDate**, and **Attendance** from the *Attendance* table, and **Lname**, **Fname** from the *Student* table.

c. Set criteria **"Absent*"** for the *Attendance* field making sure to use the * after the t.

d. Save the query as **MissedDays**. Close the query.

Create a Report That Counts the Missed Days

a. Use the Report Wizard to create a report based on the query *MissedDays*.

b. Add **Lname**, **Fname**, and **AttendDate** fields to the report design.

c. Adjust the report using the design or layout view to decrease the size of the **Lname**, **Fname** fields. Repeat for the Student Last and First Name fields in the page header section. See Figure 3.2. Move the AttendDate field in the Page Header to 4.5" mark and expand to the right 1". Rename the field Missed Days. Move the AttendDate field in the details section of the report to the 4.5" mark and expand to the right 1".

d. Title of report is **Total Missed Days by Students**. Move the Title place holder so it fits between the 2 and 6" marks. Change the font to **14 pt, Bold, Center**.

e. In the Group, Sort, and Total area at the bottom, use the More arrow to add AttendDate counted and Show in subtotal in group footer checked.

f. Remove Set the Alternate Fill/Back Color to none for middle 3 section rows. Close the Design View. See Figure 3.2, report for the design view, once you make your changes.

g. View the report. Save the report and close the report.

Update a Record Using a Form

a. With the *Guardian* table selected in the Navigation Pane, create a default form and save it as **GuardianInformation**.

b. In Design or Layout view, adjust the form as follows:
Change the font size of the form header to **22 pt, Bold**, and **Centered**.
Change the title of the form to **Guardian Information Form**.

c. Save the form.

d. Open the form and navigate to Julie Makar's record.

e. Make a note in the Notes field that reads **Will be having surgery in October and the new contact person is Nancy Makar, Aunt, at 580-234-5610.**

f. Save and close the form. Check the Guardian table for the update.

Compact, Repair, and Back Up the Database

In order to make sure your database functions as designed and is updated regularly, you need to regularly compact, repair, and back up the database especially when modifying it.

a. Compact and repair the database.

b. Back up the database in the location where you save your student files. When naming the file, include today's date. Close the database and Exit Access.

c. Submit based on instructors' direction

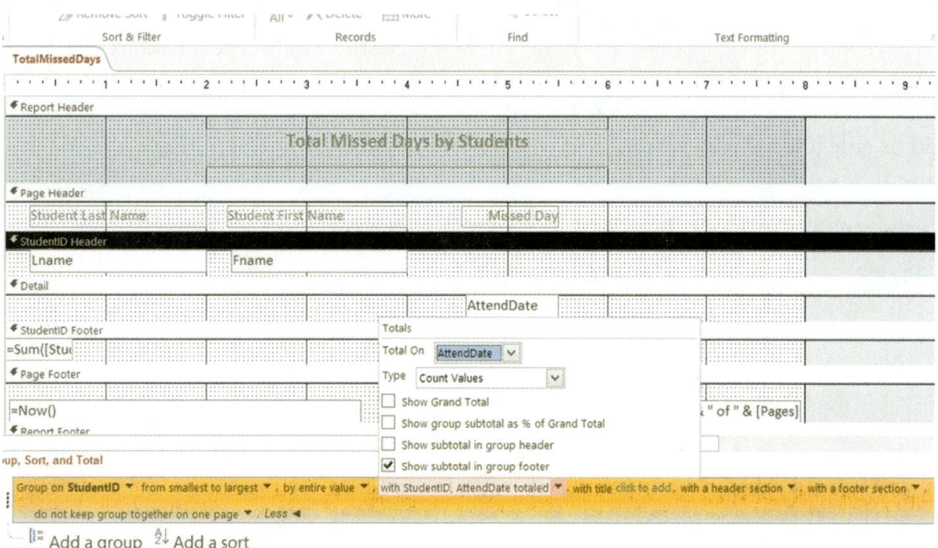

FIGURE 3.2

Use Microsoft PowerPoint

Background

People become teachers for many reasons, including an abiding interest in education. Many times teachers use multimedia presentations to engage the students with concepts and skills. PowerPoint provides a way to engage the learner through an organized approach to these presentations and the use of a full range of multimedia. In addition, with the movement to integrate technology into the classrooms and the current and developing technology standards for students, the teacher must be comfortable and skillful in using these tools to assist students in learning how to use them. Although other presentation tools are available, teachers frequently use PowerPoint as it crosses the Windows and Mac environments.

Tasks

Teachers may be responsible for using PowerPoint to prepare the following:

- Deliver lessons
- Present information to committees on various topics
- Provide presentations to parents at open house
- Review classroom rules of conduct
- Prepare presentations for use on the school's Web site or other social media sites

Skills

In addition to opening, saving, and printing a PowerPoint presentation, running a slide show, and using basic formatting, a teacher should be able to do the following:

Chapter 1

- Plan and create a presentation
- Insert media objects and tables
- Use animations and transitions
- Insert headers and footers
- Run and navigate a slide show
- Print notes page and handouts

Chapter 2

- Create a presentation using a template
- Modify a template
- Reuse slides from an existing presentation
- Modify a slide master

Chapter 3

- Create shapes
- Create SmartArt
- Create WordArt
- Modify objects
- Arrange objects

Chapter 4

- Insert a picture
- Transform a picture
- Use the Internet as a resource

Capstone Exercises

You are continuing your preparation for the start of the school year. This requires you to create several PowerPoint presentations. The first one will be a lesson orienting the students to your class. The second one will be for the open house, and the last one will be a sample lesson.

Create a New Presentation, Select a Style, and Insert a Picture

You are preparing for the first day of class. Although you can talk about all the things you want to cover, you decide to create a PowerPoint presentation to cover some of the points.

a. Open PowerPoint and create a new presentation based on the *Welcome Back to School*. Use the search feature with Welcome Back to School as the search string. Save this presentation as **03p_OrientCR_LastFirst**.

b. On the *Title* slide, replace *[Year]* with **2014-2015** or the current school year dates.

c. On *Slide 2*, replace the current title with **Agenda** and the bulleted list with **Goals, Who's Who, Classroom Rules, Field Trip, Grading, Parent Conferences**, and **Questions.**

d. Change the Slide Layout to **Two Content**. On the right side of the content area, use **Online Pictures**, the Bing Image Search, and the word **agenda**. Scroll down several rows and insert the **clipboard** with attached pencil image. Resize it to **4.48" × 5"**. Set the picture to **Transparent Color**.

Insert SmartArt and Text Box

You want to add some visual interest to Slide 3 on Goals. For many students the words aren't stimulating so you decide to use SmartArt to convey steps leading to success or achievement of goals for 8th grade.

a. Go to *Slide 3* and delete all text but *Goals* in the title placeholder. Size the title to **48 pt**. Delete the text in the content placeholder. Insert the **Step Up Process** SmartArt Graphic from the *Process Group* and type the following for the "steps." **Bold** the text in the steps.

Read and follow directions
Manage time: organize work
Take notes; document sources
Use appropriate technology for the task at hand
Strengthen writing skills
Complete work on time

b. If necessary, size the SmartArt so it looks like the slide below. Insert a text box, type **Success**, and then adjust the font size to **36** and color to **Dark Red**, **Bold**. Place it at the top of the steps as shown in Figure 3.3 Goals.

Insert Organizational Chart and Pictures

You need to create a slide that shows the organization of some key personnel for the students to start placing a face with a name and job title. Some changes have been made since last year.

a. Go to *Slide 4*. Delete the text in the content placeholder.

b. Insert the **Circle Picture Hierarchy** SmartArt Graphic from the *Hierarchy* category.

c. In the top text placeholder, type **Principal**, press **Enter**, and then type **Dr. Magnum**. Insert the 03p_Principal.jpg picture. Promote all third level items to the second level.

d. Create the following as the second level under the Principal Level. Use the Text Pane and promote all third text to second level. Use a soft return to create the second line of text after typing the first line.

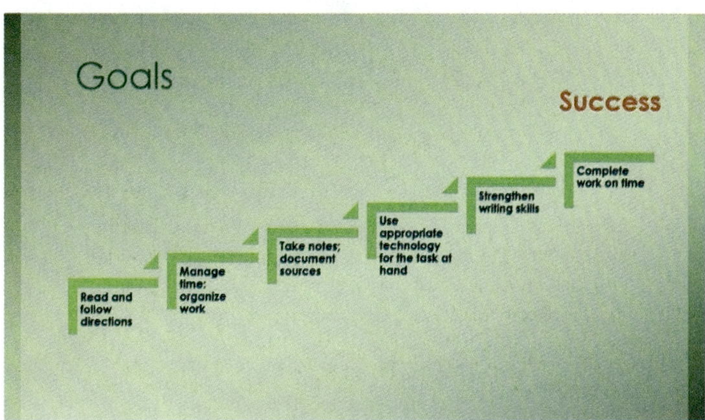

FIGURE 3.3

Type **English**, and on the second line in the text box, type **Mrs. Smith**. Insert the **03p_Smith.jpg** picture.

Type **Science**, type a soft return and on the second line in the text box, type **Mr. Alison**. Insert the **03p_Alison.jpg** picture.

Type **Social Studies**, and on the second line in the text box, type **Mr. Wagoner**. Insert the **03p_Wagoner.jpg** picture.

Type **Math**, and on the second line in the text box, type **Ms. Klosky**. Insert the **03p_Klosky.jpg** picture.

Type **Computer Lab**, and on the second line in the text box, type **Mr. Ness**. Insert the **03p_ComputerLab.jpg** picture.

Type **Librarian**, and on the second line in the text box, type **Ms. Alendar**. Insert the **03p_Librarian.jpg** picture.

e. **Bold** the text in the text pane and if necessary change the font size to **12 pt**. If necessary, make any adjustments so the area of study appears on the first line and the person's name on the second line.

Import Data from a Word Document, Pictures from Microsoft Online, and Google Images

For the next slide you want to use the classroom rules created in a Word document and add some pictures to keep students' attention while you review the rules.

a. Go to *Slide 5*. Replace the word *Policies* with **Rules** so it reads Classroom Rules. **Align Left** the title.

b. Copy the data from *03p_Rules.docx* into the content area of the slide. Move the bullet list to the right, lining up the bullets under the *C* in *Classroom*. Adjust the content placeholder on the right as necessary.

c. Insert three images from **Office.com** Clip Art online. Use the words **on time**, **no talking**, and **thank you**, respectively, for the three images. Select images that are appropriate for 8th grade. Place *on time* on the bottom left of the slide; place *no talking* above *on time*, and *thank you* above *no talking*. Now create WordArt typing the word **Respect** using **Fill - Black, Text 1, Outline - Background 1, Hard Shadow - Background 1**. Transform the WordArt to **Wave 1**. Place it on top of *thank you* so it appears on the top-left of the slide.

d. Size and line up the Clip Art as shown in Figure 3.4 Classroom Rules. Note that images may be different based on ones you selected. Use the Set Transparent Color to remove the white edges from images with them.

Change Slide Layout and Insert WordArt

Your next slide addresses a trip to Washington, D.C. You want this slide to be attention-getting so you want a large picture of the Washington, D.C., skyline with a caption. You also need to use WordArt to make sure students understand this is a trip to Washington, D.C., that highlights the major attractions.

a. Go to *Slide 6*. Change the slide layout to **Picture with Caption**.

b. Insert the **03p_DCSkyline.jpg** picture in the picture placeholder by clicking the **Pictures** icon in the placeholder.

c. In the placeholder below the picture, type **Washington D.C. Trip** for the title. **Center** the title.

d. In the bottom placeholder, type **Make sure you all participate in the fundraisers to support our class trip to Washington D.C. in November**.

e. Insert **WordArt** with a **Fill-Green Accent 3 Sharp Bevel** style on the left side of the slide. Type **Class Field Trip** rotated **Left 90°**.

Insert a Table and Symbols

Now that the students are excited about the field trip, you want to go over the grading system. You decide the cleanest approach to the grading system is to use a table and symbols to represent doing well and not so well.

a. Go to *Slide 7*. Delete the text in the content area and insert a **3 column, 7 row table**. Adjust the Table Height to **5.3"** and Width to **11.11"**.

b. Type the following information in the first two columns of the table:

Letter Grade	Percent Range
A	92–100%
B	83–91%
C	74–82%
D	65–73%
F	Below 65%
I	Incomplete

c. Use the **Wingdings Symbol** set and insert four **smiley faces** in the third column of the "A" letter row, three **smiley faces** in

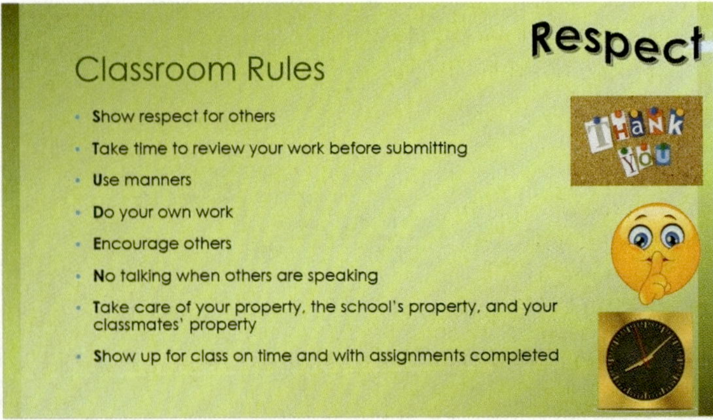

FIGURE 3.4

the "B" letter row, two **smiley faces** in the "C" letter row, one **neutral face** in the "D" letter row, and one **frown face** in the "F" letter row.

d. Adjust the faces to **32 pt** and color to **Red**. **Center** the contents of the Letter Grade column.

Insert and Adjust a Shape, WordArt, and Images

The next slide discusses the need for the students to encourage their parents to attend the parent conferences. You decide you will use a shape to highlight the major point on the slide and four images to represent the topics you will discuss.

a. Go to *Slide 8*. Delete the **Title placeholder**.

b. Insert the **Wave** shape in the title placeholder location between the ruler 5" marks horizontally and about 1" in height. Change the Shape Fill color to **Standard Color Yellow** and apply the **Gradient, Linear Up** format found in the Shape Fill, Gradient option, Dark Variations, third row, middle. Apply the Shape Effect **Bevel Circle**.

c. Insert WordArt titled **Parent Conference** and format it with **Fill - Green, Accent 2, Outline - Accent 2** (first row, third option). Change the shape to **Wave 1** (Transform, first column, Wrap area, fifth row, first item). Drag on top of the yellow shape and extend between the 4" marks on the Ruler bar. May need to display if the Ruler bar is not showing.

d. Delete the **content placeholder**. Search **Office.com** online pictures for **schedule**, **clipboard**, **parent conference**, and **email**. Insert the schedule image on the far left under the Parent Conference title. Insert the clipboard to the right of the schedule image. Next insert the parent conference and email images. These images should line up from left to right starting with schedule and ending with email. Adjust colors and size appropriately for the slide. You don't want too much white space.

e. Insert a textbox for each picture with the appropriate words— **Conference Schedule**, **Sign-Up Sheet**, **Expectations**, and **Contact via Email**. **Bold** and **Center** the text in each text box. Group each picture and related textbox together.

f. Go to *Slide 9*, remove the content placeholder, and then replace it with a **question mark** image from **Office.com**. Resize the image to fill the space from the content placeholder and remove white space on image if present. Replace the title with the word **Questions**.

g. Delete **Slide 10**. Save your file.

Insert a Footer, Add Speaker Notes, and Print the Notes Page

You now want to identify the school and slide number on each slide. You also want to insert some speaker notes to remember what you wanted to say about the slide. You notice that some of your slides are self-explanatory so you will address only those slides that require a little more explanation.

a. Insert a Footer with **Fort Pitt Middle School** in the center and **Slide number** on the right side. Exclude the title slide from the footer.

b. Go to *Slide 5 Classroom Rules*. Display the Notes pane. Open the file *03p_speakernotesrules.docx* and copy and paste the text into the Notes pane of Slide 5. So that all of your notes for this slide fit on one printed page, change the size of the text in the notes section to **12 pt**.

c. Go to *Slide 6* and type the following in the Notes pane. Set the font size to **14 pt**.

Encourage your parents to participate in the fundraisers in September and October that will make up the rest of the expenses for the field trip. We aim to cover all the costs related to transportation, hotel, food, and admissions. Your costs would be related to snacks and items you might want to purchase.

d. Go to *Slide 8* and add the following in the Notes section. Adjust the font size to **14 pt**.

Give your parents the printed copy of the parent conference schedule so they can adjust their schedules.

Your parents will need to sign up for an individual conference in addition to the open house group time.

During these conferences I will discuss our goals for 8th grade students and review expectations.

Your parents may contact me via email at asmith@fortpitt.edu.

If necessary, create a blank line between each of the four items you will cover. Save the file.

e. Print a copy of the notes pages for Slides 5, 6, and 8 and submit as directed by the instructor.

Use Animations

Now you want to add some interest to your presentation by adding some animations. This template already contains transitions, but you want to add animations to some of the slides to keep the students' interest during the class orientation.

a. Go to *Slide 5*. Select the content area and add the **Dissolve In** entrance effect.

b. Go to *Slide 8*. Select each image and apply the **Grow & Turn** entrance effect. You will have four of them.

c. Go to *Slide 9*. Apply the **Honeycomb** transition.

d. Save the file and submit as directed by the instructor. Close PowerPoint.

Integrate Microsoft Office Programs

Background

Microsoft Office applications provide the ability to integrate content from one Office program to another Office program. For example, teachers may use an outline from a Word document as a basis for a PowerPoint presentation. Teachers may import data from Access into an Excel spreadsheet or use a chart from Excel in a Word document. This ability to integrate and transfer content provides for timely completion of many of the tasks that teachers perform. In addition, teachers may also use cloud services to collaborate on projects, to review and comment on files, and to back up files.

Tasks

Microsoft Word is usually the host program for producing documents related to lesson plans, for giving information to students and parents, and for submitting papers or reports to professional organizations or administration. Microsoft PowerPoint is the program most often used for lessons and presentations given to other teachers or at conferences. Both of these programs may import information created in Excel and Access. Teachers may include the following integration tasks during the course of their teaching:

- Merge data from a student database to Word to generate custom communication documents to send to parents or to Excel to create a student grade sheet
- Embed or link Excel worksheets or charts into Word documents like newsletters and reports
- Create PowerPoint presentations with various linked or embedded objects from Word and Excel

Skills

In addition to basic formatting skills in each application program, a teacher should be able to do the following:

- Create a primary document in Word and use Access as the data source file
- Import data from Access into Excel to create the grading workbook
- Embed and link content from multiple sources into a newsletter
- Embed content from Excel into a PowerPoint presentation
- Use track changes to revise the lesson plan template
- Share the lesson plan with other teachers via OneDrive

EDUCATORS

Capstone Exercises

As you move through the first days of the academic year, you will be responsible for the communications that go to parents about the up-coming field trip, making presentations to the parents, working with the other faculty to develop a standard lesson plan template as man-dated by the school district, and producing the second newsletter. You just learned about the integration features of Microsoft Office so you will be pulling data from one application to another to make the job more efficient.

Create a Primary Document in Word and Import a Data File from Access

Your first task will be to send a personalized letter to the parents of your students requesting permission for their children to attend the field trip. You will need to create a query in Access for the fields needed for the permission letter and use the Mail Merge Wizard to create customized letters inserting the correct fields.

a. Open the Word document *03i_PermissionLetter.docx*. Save it as **03i_PermissionLetter_LastFirst**.

b. Open the Access database *03i_Students.accdb*. Save it as **03i_Students_LastFirst**.

c. In the *03i_Students_LastFirst* database, create a multiple table query using the **Guardian**, **StudentGuardian**, and **Student** tables. Set the following fields to display in the query results: from the *Student* table, fields **Lname** and **Fname**; from the *Guardian* table, fields **GuardianFirst**, **GuardianLast**, and **PrimaryGuardian**. Add criteria to display those guardians who are the primary guardian. Run the query. Save the query as **Letterimport** and close the database.

d. Go to the *03i_PersmissionLetter_LastFirst*. Use the **Step-by-Step Mail Merge Wizard** to insert the appropriate fields as listed below:
Type of document—**Letters**
Primary source—current Word document **03i_Permission-Letter_LastFirst**
Secondary data source **03i_Students_LastFirst, Letterimport** query

e. On the first page of the Word document, insert **GuardianFirst** and **GuardianLast** fields after *Dear*. Make sure you insert an appropriate blank space before the first name and between the first and last names with a comma after the salutation.

f. On the second page of the letter, insert **Fname** and **Lname** fields in the first paragraph before *has*, in the second paragraph before *requires*, and between for and to in the third paragraph. Again make sure to use appropriate spacing between first and last names. Save the file.

g. Complete the Merge, check the results, and then make any cor-rections necessary. For example, did you remember to leave a space between the first and last names? Save the merged letter as **03i_MergedPermissionLetter_LastFirst**. Close the document.

Revise the Newsletter, Embed a Chart from Excel, and Create a Bibliography/Citation

October is National Reading month and is the month the school district kicks off its yearlong reading program. You will create a bibliography reading list for the first half of the year with the rest of the list appearing in the December newsletter for the second half of the school year. You will also embed a chart from Excel to update parents on the fundraising event held in September. You want to embed the chart so if any money comes in between the times you create the newsletter and send it out, it can be updated.

a. Open the *03i_OctoberNewsletter.docx* file. Save it as **03i_OctoberNewsletter_LastFirst**.

b. Insert a **Halloween** image (row of pumpkins) from **Office.com** on the blank line below the text in the Happy Halloween text-box. Set the height to approximately 1". Enlarge the image to approximately **31/2"** and **Center** it. If there is any extra white space from around the image, remove it. There is an extra blank line below the picture, delete it.

c. In the textbox below *Update on Washington DC Field Trip and Fundraiser*, type the following:

To date, prospects look good but we still need your assistance with the October fundraiser to meet our goal of $18,300. We are short $1,681 which will need to be raised with this last fundraiser. Thanks to the parents who donated money to reach the goal of $1,500 to pay for the pool/pizza party!

Change the Font size to **10pt**. Save the document.

d. Open the file *03i_BudgetDC2014Updated.xlsx*. Save it as **03i_BudgetDC2014Update_LastFirst**.

e. Create a **3-D Clustered Column** chart that shows what was promised or raised and what was received and move the chart to its own worksheet. Add the Data label **Value** above the col-umns. Rotate the Value **Text Up**. **Bold** the Data values. Type a title for the chart: **D.C. Budget Update**.

f. Copy the chart and paste it into the newsletter on the first blank line below the text *Thanks to the parents who donated money to reach the goal of $1,500 to pay for the pool/pizza party!* Use **Paste Options, Keep Source Formatting & Embed Workbook.** Size the chart so it stays on the first page. It should be about 21/2" high by 5" wide. Center the chart within the textbox if necessary.

g. Below the text in *Important Announcements*, insert an image of books from **Office.com**. Size the image to about 2" by 2". This image should stay on the first page and not cover the page number.

h. The first page should look something like Figure 3.5. The pumpkin and book images will vary depending on the ones you selected.

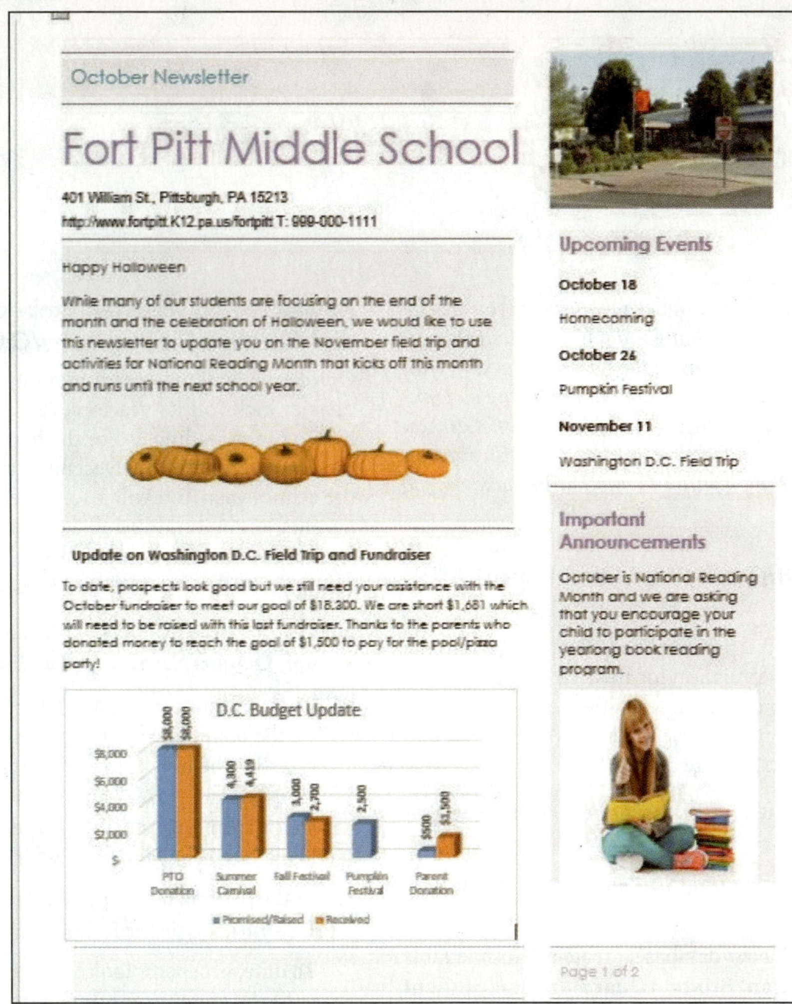

FIGURE 3.5

i. On the second page, under the heading *National Book Reading Month*, type the following:

This month starts the first month of the school's book reading program to coincide with National Book Reading Month. The 8th grade teachers and the Librarian prepared this list for you to review as possibilities for your child. While it is acceptable to select any book you approve for your child to read, we will be providing additional suggestions in upcoming newsletters. Of course, the Librarian can help your child select a book that will peak your child's interest in reading.

j. Set the Style to **APA**. Create bibliographical entries using **Manage Sources**—Book Section. Type the following:

Author	Title	Year	Publisher
Orson Scott Card	Ender's Game	2010	Tor Science Fiction
Jane Leslie Conly	Crazy Lady	1995	Laura Geringer Books
Robert Cormier	The Chocolate War	1974	Random House
S.E. Hinton	The Outsiders	2006	SPEAK

Author	Title	Year	Publisher
Jon Krakauer	Into the Wild	2009	Anchor Books
J.R.R. Tolkien	The Hobbit	2001	Houghton Mifflin

k. Make sure these authors are added to the current list in the Source Manager. Insert these authors into the newsletter below the paragraph just typed using Insert Citation.

l. Using a search engine, find two quotes about reading and insert them starting on a blank line below the suggested book list, for example: "I find television very educating. Every time somebody turns on the set, I go into the other room and read a book," Groucho Marx ("Quotes About Reading," n.d.); or "The more that you read, the more things you will know. The more that you learn, the more places you'll go," Dr. Seuss, *I Can Read With My Eyes Shut!* ("Quotes About Reading, n.d.) Add the site to the bibliography created in j and update the bibliography. After the quote, include a citation listing the source of the quotes. Apply the Quotes Style to the quotation and citation.

m. Replace the picture on page 2 with the *ReadingBooks.jpg* file. Undo the Lock Aspect Ratio and enlarge to a height of 2.05" and a width of 2.38". In the More Important News section of

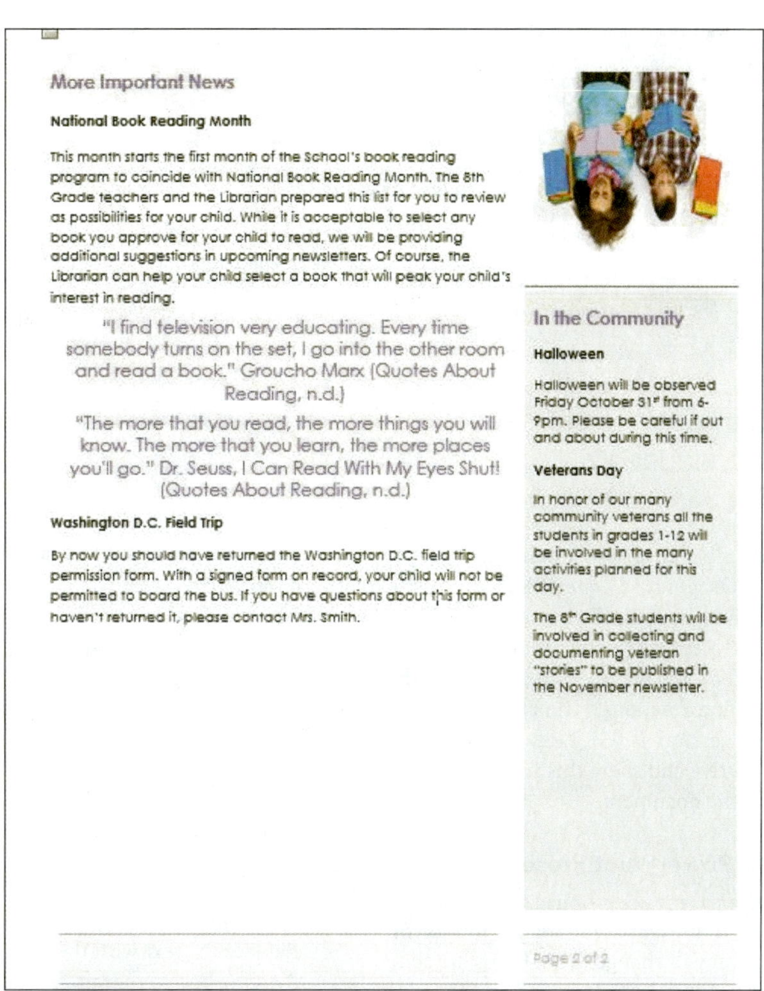

More Important News

National Book Reading Month

This month starts the first month of the School's book reading program to coincide with National Book Reading Month. The 8th Grade teachers and the Librarian prepared this list for you to review as possibilities for your child. While it is acceptable to select any book you approve for your child to read, we will be providing additional suggestions in upcoming newsletters. Of course, the Librarian can help your child select a book that will peak your child's interest in reading.

"I find television very educating. Every time somebody turns on the set, I go into the other room and read a book." Groucho Marx (Quotes About Reading, n.d.)

"The more that you read, the more things you will know. The more that you learn, the more places you'll go." Dr. Seuss, I Can Read With My Eyes Shut! (Quotes About Reading, n.d.)

Washington D.C. Field Trip

By now you should have returned the Washington D.C. field trip permission form. With a signed form on record, your child will not be permitted to board the bus. If you have questions about this form or haven't returned it, please contact Mrs. Smith.

In the Community

Halloween

Halloween will be observed Friday October 31ª from 6-9pm. Please be careful if out and about during this time.

Veterans Day

In honor of our many community veterans all the students in grades 1-12 will be involved in the many activities planned for this day.

The 8ᵗʰ Grade students will be involved in collecting and documenting veteran "stories" to be published in the November newsletter.

Page 2 of 2

FIGURE 3.6

the newsletter, page 2, go to the end and press the Enter key. Set the style to Normal and type:

Washington, D.C., Field Trip

By now you should have returned the Washington, D.C., field trip permission form. With a signed form on record, your child will not be permitted to board the bus. If you have questions about this form or haven't returned it, please contact Mrs. Smith.

Bold the title. The second page should look like Figure 3.6.

Save the file. Close the document.

Use Track Changes, Insert Comments, and Share a Document

Mr. Wagoner decided to share a lesson plan template he uses for his courses. You decide that the best way for the 8th grade teachers to revise this template is by using OneDrive. The goal is to create one template that all four of the 8th grade teachers can use. This will help with consistency in applying the standards required by the State Board of Education. Your first task will be to open the document from Mr. Wagoner and add your comments to it. You will then upload your commented document to OneDrive and invite your professor to view it.

a. Open the *03i_LessonPlanOriginal.docx* file and save it as **03i_LessonPlanOriginal_LastFirst**.

b. Make the following comments in the document.

Insert a comment for *[For example, Internet: Searching for Quality Information]* that reads **Should we place a note here to replace what is in brackets for each new lesson?**

Insert a comment for *Objectives* that reads **Should we include a reference note here saying we use Bloom's Taxonomy?**

Insert a comment for a *coverage* that reads **I believe we need a section break, next page here to keep the preliminary information separate from the actual plan details.**

c. Save the document with the comments. Access your OneDrive account. Create a folder called **lessonplan** and upload the **03i_LessonPlanOriginal_LastFirst** file to the *lessonplan* folder in your OneDrive account. Close the document.

d. Share this file with your professor and give the professor access to change It. Type a note in the comment text block:

Take a look at this Lesson Plan Template. Make comments and revisions as necessary. Rename the file by adding your initials to the end. Please post revisions by August 1st so we can have this ready for the start of the school year.

School Policies

- How the school addresses academic and behavioral problems
- School's policies regarding tardiness, absence, and discipline can be found on the school's website http://www.fortpitt.K12.pa.us
- Additional Information:
  - School cancellations for bad weather and other reasons
  - Emergency procedures
  - Transportation
  - After-school activities
  - Volunteering

FIGURE 3.7

e. A few days later, you download and save a marked-up copy. Open the *03i_LessonPlanOriginal_MS.docx* file. Review the comments and accept all changes made. Delete the comments. Add a footnote with the text **Replace the text in brackets with the appropriate text based on the lesson plan topic** after the top bracketed text [Quality Information]. Format the first page as portrait. Save the final version as **03i_LessonPlanFinal_LastFirst**. Upload to OneDrive and share this final document with your professor. Close the document.

Develop an Open House PowerPoint Presentation

You are now preparing for the parent open house held each fall. You will be using PowerPoint to present some major points you want to make to the parents. You will change the color of the slide master, check each slide for potential changes due to the color change, and reuse selected slides from a student classroom orientation presentation.

a. Open *03i_ParentOpenHouse.pptx* and save the file as **03i_ParentOpenHouse_LastFirst**.

b. Change the *Slide Master Theme Colors* to **Orange Red**.

c. On *Slide 1*, change the subtitle color to **Orange, Accent 1**.

d. On *Slide 4*, copy and paste the English WordArt creating Math, Science, Social Studies, and Electives subjects. Change the colors as follows: Math = **Yellow**, Science = **Dark Red**, Social Studies = **Green**, and Electives = **Purple**. Arrange the WordArt around the slide.

e. Replace *Slide 5* with **Slide 3 Grading** from the *03i_POrientation.pptx* presentation. Change the table style to **Light Style 2 - Accent 2** in the Light section, second row, third column).

f. Replace *Slide 6* with **Slide 2 Classroom Rules** from *03i_POrientation.pptx* presentation.

g. Edit the text on *Slide 7* to match the text in Figure 3.7 School Policies.

   Change the Title text to **Black**.

h. Go to *Slide 8*. Change the color of the Title text to **Black, Bold**. Replace the text with the following:
   Reading book program
   Lunch room monitors
   Fundraisers for class field trip to Washington, D.C.
   Eliminate hunger campaign
   PTO (Parent Teacher Organization)

i. On *Slide 9* delete the content placeholder. Insert a text box typing **?**. Change the font to **80 pt** and the color **Dark Red, Accent 2**. Make 4 copies of the ? and randomly scatter on the slide.

j. Save and submit based on instructors' direction. Close the presentation and exit PowerPoint.

Legal Discipline

Using Microsoft Office as a Paralegal

BACKGROUND | Working as a Paralegal

The abundance of paperwork in a law office requires much use of word processors. A Paralegal's work involves creating, modifying and disseminating legal documents. The applications in Microsoft Office aid the Paralegal in formatting documents to have a professional appearance, in both paper and electronic form. An electronic spreadsheet can be used to record client fees, client deposits, as well as to set up and/or monitor trust accounts. The Paralegal may be responsible for tracking all phases of the law office operation by storing and maintaining the information in a database.

Attorneys today use multimedia in the courtroom for trial openings, closings, and as a supplement to a formal presentation. Paralegals and legal assistants may be responsible for doing research and developing the presentation. A flyer can also be generated using data from the presentation file or a chart created from data in the electronic spreadsheet.

Discipline-Specific Capstones

Using Office in the Legal Profession

Application	Exercises	Skills Covered
1. WORD Data Files: 04w_Facts 04w_Saww Solution Files: 04w_Facts_LastFirst 04w_Saww_LastFirst	WORKERS' COMPENSATION (page 73)	• Insert headers and footers • Check spelling and grammar • Insert nonbreaking space • Set margins • Modify document properties • Add page numbers (p. 128) • Modify paragraph spacing • Select indents. • Apply styles • Insert a picture • Resize and move a picture • Modify a picture • Create a table • Insert a row • Apply a table style • Adjust table position and alignment • Format table text • Calculate using table formulas • Acknowledge a source • Add legal references • Create footnotes • Insert a cover page • Add a comment • View and deactivate a comment • Accept changes
2. EXCEL Data Files: 04e_Trust Solution Files: 04e_Ledger_LastFirst 04e_Trust_LastFirst	CLIENT AND TRUST LEDGERS (page 77)	• Design a worksheet • Enter and edit cell data • Use cell references in a formula • Apply the order of precedence • Copy formulas with auto fill • Rename worksheets • Copy worksheets • Insert columns and rows • Adjust column width • Hide and unhide columns and rows • Select a range • Copy and paste a range • Use Paste Special • Merge and center labels • Apply alignment and font options • Apply number formats • Set page orientation • Set margin options • Create a footer • Use relative, absolute, and mixed cell references • Insert the TODAY function • Use the IF function • Use the VLOOKUP function • Create nested functions • Create a bar chart • Select the data source • Move a chart • Apply a chart layout and a chart style • Format data labels • Freeze rows and columns • Create a table • Apply a table style • Apply a number filter • Add a total row
3. ACCESS Data Files: 04a_ImportCases.xlsx Solution Files: 04a_LawFirm_LastFirst	CLIENT AND CASE TRACKING (page 81)	• Navigate among the objects in an Access database • Add and edit records • Back up, compact, and repair Access files • Sort table data on one or more fields • Use and remove a filter • Understand relational power • Use the Relationships window • Enforce referential integrity • Create a database • Design a table • Create and modify tables • Understand table relationships • Import and Excel spreadsheet • Establish table relationships • Create a single-table query • Use query design view • Specify criteria in a query for different data types • Run, copy, and modify a query • Create a multitable query • Modify a multitable query • Create a calculated field in a query • Format and save calculated results • Verify calculated results • Create expressions with the Expression Builder • Use built-in functions in Access • Create a totals query with grouping • Create forms using form tools • Modify a form • Revise forms using Layout view • Identify control types in forms • Create reports using the Report Wizard • Modify a report • Revise reports using Layout and Design views • Identify control types in reports

4. POWERPOINT	BANKRUTPCY BASICS (page 85)	• Plan a presentation • Use slide layouts • Create a new presentation • Add new slides • Use spell check • Apply themes • Insert media objects • Add a table • Use transitions and animations • Run and navigate a slide show • Import an outline • Modify a theme • Convert text to a SmartArt diagram • Modify objects • Arrange objects • Insert a picture • Transform a picture • Use the Internet as a resource • Add video • Use video tools
Data Files: 04p_Outline.rtf 04p_LawBooks.jpg 04p_Relief.jpg Solution Files: 04p_Bankruptcy_LastFirst		
5. INTEGRATED	JUDICIAL CAMPAIGN MATERIALS (page 88)	• Create and utilize a database containing contact information • Create a merge source file • Format a worksheet • Create a chart in Excel • Embed and link content from multiple sources • Choose records or fields to merge • Create a flyer • Create a presentation file
Data Files: 04i_ContactInfo.xlsx 04i_Letter.docx 04i_Responses.xlsx 04i_Dewitt.tif Solution Files: 04i_Contacts_solution.accdb 04i_Letter_LastFirst.docx 04i_Responses_LastFirst.xlsx 04i_Merge_solution.docx 04i_Flyer_solution.pptx 04i_Fair_solution.pptx		

Use Microsoft Word

Background

Word processors are the most used application program in a law office. Paralegals help create, modify, and disseminate a wide variety of legal documents. It is imperative that the paralegal knows the many features available in Microsoft Word and is comfortable using them without having to refer back regularly to a reference guide. Occasionally, however, the paralegal may need to refer to Microsoft Office Help to gain the knowledge needed to complete an unfamiliar task. The skills you use to complete the following tasks are taught in the four Word chapters and are all vital paralegal skills. In addition, you may want to use Microsoft Office Help to refresh your knowledge or to learn about more advanced skills.

Tasks

In a small office, the paralegal may be responsible for all kinds of document production. This could include the following:

- Correspondence and mailings (cover letters, fact sheets, and copies of pleadings)
- Presentations
- Forms, including billing
- Memoranda
- Reports and briefs

In a larger office, the office assistant may take care of general typing duties, but the paralegal might still be responsible for the following:

- Pleadings
- Research
- Case documentation

Skills

In addition to basic formatting skills, a paralegal should be able to do the following:

Chapter 1

- Insert headers and footers
- Check spelling and grammar
- Insert nonbreaking space
- Set margins
- Modify document properties
- Add page numbers

Chapter 2

- Modify paragraph spacing
- Select indents.
- Apply styles
- Insert a picture
- Resize and move a picture
- Modify a picture

Chapter 3

- Create a table
- Insert a row
- Apply a table style
- Adjust table position and alignment
- Format table text
- Calculate using table formulas

Chapter 4

- Acknowledge a source
- Add legal references
- Create footnotes
- Insert a cover page
- Add a comment
- View and deactivate a comment
- Accept changes

PARALEGALS

Capstone Exercises

You work for a workers' compensation attorney who will be making a presentation at a state bar function. Your boss wants to prepare a document to share with the attendees that will highlight the way workers' compensation intersects with other areas of law. You have been provided with a copy of his document to format, but it contains comments from one of his colleagues who reviewed the document. Prepare this document so that it has a professional appearance. It will be distributed in both paper and electronic form, so you will prepare it for appropriate viewing by either method.

Accept Document Revisions

You review the document comments made by your attorney's colleague and notice that she has used a combination of methods to insert her suggestions. Your attorney has already authorized you to accept the revisions and apply her suggestions to his document.

a. Open *04w_Facts* and save it as **04w_Facts_LastFirst**.

b. Review the document in All Markup Tracking mode to see what kinds of changes and comments have been made. Accept all changes and stop tracking document revisions in this document.

c. Delete all of the comments that were inserted throughout the document.

Use Find and Replace Commands

With the Show/Hide (¶) feature active to check spacing of headings, you note that in several locations there are two spaces between words and after periods instead of the correct single space. While scanning the document, you also note that a contraction was used, and you wish to change it to the more formal legal style, which does not use contractions.

a. Turn on the **Show/Hide (¶) feature**, if you have not already done so. Then move the cursor to the top of the document.

b. Use the Replace feature to locate two spaces and replace with one space. Review each spacing located and update accordingly.

c. Use the Replace feature to search for the contraction *don't* and replace with **do not**.

Apply Styles and Use Format Painter

Review the outline of the document to see how it is formatted. You decide to format the title, author's name, and each paragraph heading. The paragraph and section headings in the document are currently written using the normal style, with individually applied attributes (such as bold). Use the existing Heading 1 style to reformat the headings.

a. Apply the **Book Title style** to the title of the document. Modify the style to use a font size of **16 pt**.

b. Select the **author identification line**. Apply the **Emphasis style**.

c. Select the first-level paragraph heading *Generally* and apply the **Heading 1 style**.

d. Use the Format Painter to apply this style to the remaining first-level paragraph headings.

Modify Styles

The attorney prefers a more traditional color scheme, so you modify the Heading 1 style. You also modify the Normal style to include a first line indent.

a. Right-click the **Heading 1 style** in the Styles group on the HOME tab and click **Modify** to open the Modify Style dialog box. Modify the Heading 1 style so the font color applied is **Dark Blue, Text 2, Darker 50%.**

b. Click **Format** in the Modify Style dialog box and modify the Paragraph format to include **6 pt** spacing after. Click **OK** to close the Modify Style dialog box.

c. Modify the Normal style to include a First line Indent. Click **OK** to close the Paragraph dialog box and click **OK** to close the Modify Style dialog box.

Format the Document

You want the document to be formal yet appealing. Apply additional formatting features to improve the appearance.

a. Set the left and right document margins to **1.5"**.

b. Insert a header using the Insight style which is found in the selection *More Headers from Office.com*.

c. Click the **Document Title placeholder** and type the header text **Workers' Compensation: A Few Facts Worth Knowing for the Non-Practitioner**.

d. Adjust the First Line Indent on the vertical ruler so it is set at the margin. Align the header text to the left margin.

e. Insert a footer using the Insight style. The Insight style automatically includes the page number at the right margin.

f. Adjust the First Line Indent on the vertical ruler so it is set at the left margin. Align the footer to the left margin.

g. Press **backspace** twice to move to the left margin and type the author's name, **Robert J. MacDonald**. Insert a right tab at the right margin for the placement of the page number and press **Tab** to move the page number. Close the *Header/Footer* section.

Apply a Non-Breaking Space

You review the document to see how the formatting changes you made impacted line and paragraph endings. You notice on the top of page 3 in the *Family Law* section that the MCL in the second paragraph is on one line and the actual number of the law is on the next line. You fix that by applying a non-breaking space between the parts. (The MCL will move to the next line.)

a. Insert a non-breaking space between *MCL* and *552.625a(6)(d)*. Use the Find feature to locate this reference, if necessary.

b. Remove the existing space between *MCL* and the non-breaking space.

Add a Picture

Add a picture to the top of the document and position the image on the right side of the page. Add a picture style to the image.

a. Press **Ctrl+Home** to place the insertion point at the beginning of the document. Insert an online picture at the beginning of the document. Type **crutches** in the Office.com **Clip Art Search box** and press enter. Choose the solid colored clip art image of a man standing with two crutches or any other similar image and insert it into the document.

b. Change the height of the graphic to **1"**, allowing the width to change proportionately.

c. Change the position of the image to **Position in Top Right with Square Text Wrapping**.

d. Apply the **Snip Diagonal Corner, White picture style** to the image.

Add a Footnote

The author's credentials are currently located at the end of the document. You decide to position the qualifications in a footnote on the first page.

a. Locate the Editor's Note at the end of the document and cut the italicized paragraph so it is copied to the Clipboard.

b. Move your insertion point behind the author's name on the first page of the document. Add a footnote. Paste the paragraph containing the author's credentials so it appears as the footnote on the bottom of the first page.

Insert a Cover Page and Change the Theme Colors

As this document will be distributed at the State Bar meeting, it would be more professional to include a cover page. Because consistency gives a professional appearance, use the Semaphore format to create the cover page. Your boss also likes the color blue, so you format the document with a blue color scheme.

a. Move to the top of your document.

b. Create a cover page using the Semaphore style.

c. Complete the cover page information:

- Change the date to **9/23/2015**.

- The title should be in place. If not, copy the title from the header of your document.

- Delete the subtitle.

- Change the author's name from *EXPLORING SERIES* to **Robert J. MacDonald**. Modify the font of the author's name to remove the All Caps feature.

- Change the company name to **MacDonald, FitzGerald & MacDonald, PC**.

- Delete the company address content control.

d. Make a copy of your graphic from page 2. Click before the page break at the top of the cover page and paste.

e. Use the Layout Options to set the Absolute Position for Horizontal to **2.1"** and Vertical to **1.0"**. Change the image size to a height of **4.8"**. Click **OK** to close the Layout dialog box.

f. Open the theme colors and choose the **Blue Warm color scheme** for the document. (Note: Change only the theme colors, not the document theme.)

Mark Citations and Add a Table of Authorities

A Table of Authorities references cases, rules, treaties, and other documents referred to in a legal document. You will create a Table of Authorities for this article. The Table of Authorities will be positioned at the end of the article, although the typical location of a Table of Authorities is at the beginning of a legal document. Your Table of Authorities is positioned at the end because it is not actually part of the article. You will locate and mark only the citations on the first page of the article.

a. Move to the first paragraph of the document. Locate the text *MCL 418.101-941*. Select the full text of the citation, beginning with *Michigan Workers'* and ending with the case number. Be careful not to include any extra characters or punctuation in the selection.

b. Click the **REFERENCES tab** and click **Mark Citation** in the *Table of Authorities* group. The selected text appears at the top of the dialog box. Mark this citation in the Statutes category. Click **Mark** and close the dialog box. The citation will appear within the paragraph.

c. Mark the following as citations to be included in the Table of Authorities:

Statutes:

IRC 104(a)(2)

Other Authorities:

IRS Publication 907

Cases:

Radecki v. Worker's Disability Compensation Director, 208 Mich App 19; 526 NW2d 611 (1994)

d. Move to the end of the document. Insert a page break if the page is not blank.

e. Type the title **Table of Authorities** and format it with **Heading 1 style**. Insert two blank lines.

f. Insert a Table of Authorities. Accept all defaults in the dialog box.

Add a Document Comment

You need to get the attorney's approval for the citation format in the Table of Authorities. You add a comment to the article with this request before sending the article to him.

a. Insert the following as a comment on the Table of Authorities page: **Please check the formatting of the Table of Authorities' citations. If it appears as you want, I will mark the rest of the citations.**

Update Document Properties

It is important to develop the habit of using the document properties feature for your law office documents. Even though this document will be used for outside presentations, your office enforces the standard of always using the document properties.

a. Open the **Document Panel** and update the information. You may retype the information or copy and paste it from other locations in the document, as needed.

- Author: **Robert J. MacDonald**
- Title: **Workers' Compensation: A Few Facts Worth Knowing for the Non-Practitioner**
- Subject: **WC overview for Attys**
- Keywords: **WC, General, Attorney**
- Category: **Presentation**
- Status: **Completed**
- Comments: **Prepared for State Bar presentation, Sept 23, 2015. Formatted by <your name>**

b. Close the Document Panel.

Check Spelling and Grammar

Although a legal document contains many abbreviations and legal terms that may not be in the standard dictionary, a paralegal should still check a legal document for spelling and grammar errors. As standard abbreviations and terms are discovered, they should be added to the Custom Dictionary.

a. Save your document and run the spelling checker.

b. Correct all misspelled words.

c. Click **Ignore All** when prompted to change the abbreviation *Mich.*

d. Save the document. Close the document but do not exit Microsoft Word.

Create a Table

In addition to the article, the attorney plans to distribute a table showing the Michigan State average weekly wages for the past five years.

a. Open a new document and save the document as **04w_Saww_LastFirst**.

b. Create a table with six columns and six rows.

c. Enter the following information from Table 4.1.

d. Insert a footer using the Insight style. Type **Source: Michigan State Workers' Compensation Agency**.

e. Apply **Align Left** to move the text to the left margin. Place the insertion point in front of the page number and set a **right align tab** at the right margin. Press **Tab** to right align the page number.

Format a Table

You format the table to make it easier to read and give it a more professional appearance.

a. Insert a new row above the row containing the column headings. Merge the cells in the new row and enter the table title: **State Average Weekly Wage Chart**. Bold the title and change the font size to **22 pt**.

b. Apply the **Grid Table 5 Dark - Accent - 5** table style to the table.

c. Bold the column headings and change the font size to **12 pt**. Repeat the process with the years in the first column.

d. Change the alignment for the column headings to **Align Bottom Center**.

e. Set the alignment for rows 3 through 7 to **Align Top Center**.

f. Drag the table down to give blank room at the top of the page.

Apply Text Effects to a Title

You will create an eye-catching title for the page with the table using Text Effects.

a. Cick outside the table and then press **Ctrl+Home** to move the insertion point to the beginning of the document.

a. Type **Michigan Workers' Compensation** at the top of the page and apply the **Gradient Fill-Blue, Accent 1, Reflection text effect**.

b. Apply the **Offset Diagonal Bottom Right style** to adjust the Shadow text effect.

c. Change the font size to **22 pt**.

d. Center the title horizontally on the page.

Save the Document

Now that you have made significant changes to the document, you want to be sure and save your work.

a. Save the document **04w_Saww_LastFirst**. Close the document.

b. Exit the program and submit the two documents based on your instructor's directions.

Year	SAWW	90% of SAWW (Maximum)	66% of SAWW	50% of SAWW (Minimum Benefit for Death Cases)	25% of SAWW (Minimum Benefit for Specific Loss and T&P)
2013	$820.04	$738.04	$541.23	$410.02	$205.01
2012	$803.17	$722.85	$530.09	$401.59	$200.79
2011	$784.31	$705.88	$517.64	$392.16	$196.08
2010	$765.12	$688.61	$504.98	$382.56	$191.28
2009	$744.49	$670.04	$491.36	$372.25	$186.12

TABLE 4.1

Use Microsoft Excel

Background

Microsoft Excel is such a versatile program that an experienced paralegal can find many valuable uses for Excel in the law office. Rather than knowing only a prescribed list of traditional uses, a paralegal should be alert to possible creative uses of Excel.

One of the tasks for which a paralegal may be responsible is recording transactions related to a trust account. A trust account is an account established by the lawyer and law firm for recording client fees and deposits. Each state has its own rules for trust account formatting and processing. For example, in Michigan, the distinction between retainer and advance fees has recently been clarified, and the distinction imposes some additional accounting requirements on the law office. Because a paralegal might be the person designated to set up and/or monitor the trust account, an accounting topic has been chosen for this exercise, even though many law offices use other programs for accounting purposes.

Tasks

In a small office, the paralegal may be responsible for all kinds of worksheet tasks, including the following:

- Completing accounting tasks
- Tracking client expenditures in a case
- Calculating probate expenses
- Determining real estate closure costs
- Preparing charts as trial exhibits

Skills

In addition to basic formatting skills, a paralegal should be able to do the following:

Chapter 1

- Design a worksheet
- Enter and edit cell data
- Use cell references in a formula
- Apply the order of precedence
- Copy formulas with auto fill
- Rename worksheets
- Copy worksheets
- Insert columns and rows
- Adjust column width
- Hide and unhide columns and rows
- Select a range
- Copy and paste a range
- Use Paste Special
- Merge and center labels
- Apply alignment and font options
- Apply number formats
- Set page orientation
- Set margin options
- Create a footer

Chapter 2

- Use relative, absolute, and mixed cell references
- Insert the TODAY function
- Use the IF function
- Use the VLOOKUP function
- Create nested functions

Chapter 3

- Create a bar chart
- Select the data source
- Move a chart
- Apply a chart layout and a chart style
- Format data labels

Chapter 4

- Freeze rows and columns
- Create a table
- Apply a table style
- Apply a number filter
- Add a total row

Capstone Exercises

An attorney in your office recently attended a continuing legal education seminar that emphasized the need for individual client tracking on a trust account. Although you had maintained a trust ledger, you had not been providing individual client ledgers. (Some professionals recommend having a ledger for every client, regardless of whether any of the client's funds are in the trust account!) While designing the worksheets, you realized that you could create the individual client ledgers and then construct the trust ledger as a set of links from the client ledgers. Just as Microsoft creates templates that can be used over and over again, you can create the individual client ledger as a template and use it for each client of the attorney.

Create a Client Ledger

As you plan the worksheet to be used as the template for the individual client ledgers, you determine the information you need to record and decide each type of information should be identified with a column label. When the attorney takes a case, the client pays a retainer for the attorney's services. This creates a deposit that is added to the account. If the attorney returns funds to a client, a check is issued, which is subtracted from the account. After planning the worksheet for use as the template, you create and name it. You will format the workbook so that all worksheets based on the template look alike.

a. Create a new workbook and save it as **04e_Ledger_LastFirst**.

b. Type the worksheet title **Client Ledger** in **cell A1**. Type an asterisk in **cell A2**, as the subtitle (this * in the cell is used as a placeholder for the client's name). Apply **16 pt size** and bold to the **range A1:A2**.

c. Merge and center the **ranges A1:J1** and **A2:J2**.

d. Type **Case #** in **cell A3** and apply bold.

e. Type the following labels on row 5:

   - **DATE** in **cell A5**
   - **CLIENT** in **cell B5**
   - **SOURCE OF DEPOSIT** in **cell C5**
   - **PAYEE** in **cell D5**
   - **CK #** in **cell E5**
   - **PURPOSE** in **cell F5**
   - **CHECKS (SUBTRACT)** in **cell G5**
   - **DEPOSITS (ADD)** in **cell H5**
   - **RUNNING BALANCE** in **cell I5**
   - **MEMO** in **cell J5**

f. Format the labels on row 5 with **12 pt**. Apply **Wrap Text**, **Top Align**, and **Center** alignments. Adjust column widths as needed so that labels such as *SOURCE OF DEPOSIT* display on two lines within the respective cell.

g. Apply the **Short Date format** to the **range A6:A30**.

h. Apply the **Text format** to the **range B6:F30**.

i. Apply the **Accounting Number Format** to the **range G6:I30**.

j. Format the **range A5:J30** as a table. Select the option that indicates your table has headers. Apply the **Table Style Light 2 format** to the table.

k. Add a Total Row.

l. Change the zoom to **75%** if columns A through J do not display onscreen.

m. Rename the worksheet tab of Sheet1 to **Client Template**.

Change the Page Layout

Set the print options for this ledger template so that worksheets created from the template are ready to be printed and inserted into the client's file. Due to the amount of information, you will change the format so that the worksheet prints in landscape orientation.

a. Set the page orientation to **Landscape**.

b. Set the Print Area to the **range A1:J31**.

c. Use Print Preview to check that all columns display on one page.

d. Click the **HOME tab**.

Create the Formulas for the Ledger

You have created this worksheet as a template for individual client ledgers. Just as you applied formats to the template, you create formulas in the template.

a. Type **Beginning Balance** in **cell F6** and adjust the column width. Enter **0** in **cell I6**. Note that the *0* changes to a hyphen and a *$* appears because it displays in Accounting Number Format.

b. Create a formula in **cell I7** that calculates the running balance after that row's transaction. The formula needs to subtract the check amount from and add the deposit amount to the running balance. Use the fill handle to copy the formula down the table column to **cell I30**.

c. Review the total row, with totals for the CHECKS and DEPOSITS columns. Remove the total from the Memo column.

Create an Individual Client Ledger

Make a copy of the worksheet template containing the individual client ledger. Use it to set up a ledger for a new client

a. Create a copy of the Client Template worksheet. Change the worksheet tab name from *Client Template (2)* to your name.

b. Replace the asterisk (*) in the subtitle row with your name.

c. Use Figure 4.1 to enter information about your account in the ledger. The column I totals will automatically appear as you complete columns G and H. Adjust column widths to improve the appearance of the worksheet.

d. Create a footer with the sheet name code on the left side and the file name code on the right side of each worksheet.

e. Set **0.2"** left and right margins and scale to fit to one page for the second worksheet.

f. Save and close the workbook. Submit based on your instructor's directions.

Insert a Nested Function

Once the client ledgers have been set up and entries recorded, you make a trust ledger to consolidate all of the entries into one large document. This process would need to be automated if you had many clients, and you would probably use a specialized program. In this small office, however, you can create the trust ledger using Excel. You need to be extremely careful using this process so that you do not introduce errors.

The template you created in the previous activity has been modified to include additional columns and revised column headings. Client ledgers have been created based on the template, and the template has been used to create a new worksheet titled Trust Ledger, Linda Ron, P.C. You enter the formulas for the trust ledger.

a. Open *04e_Trust* and save it as **04e_Trust_LastFirst**.

b. Change the title of the Trust Ledger worksheet by replacing the attorney name in **cell A1**, *Linda Ron*, with **your name**.

c. Type **5000** in **cell K12** for the running balance (the amount from the end of the previous period).

d. Create a nested AND function within an IF function in **cell K13**: If the fees, charges, and payment received are each zero, display nothing by using "", (two quotation marks without any text, values, or formulas in between). This logical test detects the end of the transactions and will not repeat the same balance for rows that do not have transactions. Otherwise, add the previous row's running balance to the payment received and subtract fees and charges to get the new running balance. Use Help to learn how to nest the AND function in an IF function. The goal is to have the balance display if a balance exists but have empty cells in the running balance if it is the end of the entries. Copy this formula down the column to **cell K36**. Enter and copy this same function in the other worksheets. Note: You will see a #VALUE error in a cell where the formula is waiting for input to the other parts of the worksheet to show a valid value.

e. Insert today's date by function in **cell I3** on the Trust Ledger sheet.

Use the IF and VLOOKUP Functions

To help identify the type of fees charged to a client, a table was inserted at the top of each of the ledgers identifying the administrative fee code, an explanation of the fees, and the administrative fee charge. The ledgers include a column identifying the fee code and a column displaying the fee charged based on the code. Using the IF and VLOOKUP functions, you create the formula to have Excel search the table for the type of fee and return the value for that fee. In addition, if there is no fee type specified in the ledger, the value returned should be a hyphen (-).

a. Display the Coolin, Tracey worksheet.

b. Create a nested VLOOKUP function within an IF function in **cell H13**. If the Admin Fees Type cell is empty for that row, display a zero. In the value_if_false argument, nest a VLOOKUP function that looks up the administrative fee code in **cell G13**, compares it to the lookup table in the range G6:I9, and then returns the administrative fee. (Note: Use absolute and relative cell references appropriately.)

c. Copy the administrative fees formula down the column to **cell H36**.

d. Enter the same nested function from **cell H13** in the Grab, Mark; Mattox, Brian; and Client Template worksheets and copy them down the table columns.

Enter the Data

You will create links from the original client ledgers to the trust ledger. By making links, subsequent changes to the client ledgers will show up in the trust ledger. Note: New entries will still have to be copied manually. Although you are familiar with copying cell contents to the Clipboard, creating links with the content of the cell may be unfamiliar to you. Before completing this portion of the activity, review the Help topic Copy specific cell contents or attributes in a worksheet.

a. Select the **Coolin, Tracey worksheet**. Select the **range A13:J19** (the completed rows but not the starter row). Copy the information.

b. Switch to the Trust Ledger worksheet. Select **cell A13**, the first empty row after the starter row.

c. Use the Paste Link option to link the pasted cells.

d. Copy the **range L13:L19** from the Coolin, Tracey worksheet and use the Paste Link option to link the pasted cells, starting in **cell L13** in the Trust Ledger worksheet.

e. Repeat steps a–d above with the Grab, Mark and Mattox, Brian worksheets. Paste each worksheet data below Tracey Coolin's data in the Trust Ledger worksheet.

	A	B	C	D	E	F	G	H	I	J
1						Client Ledger				
2						Student Name				
3	Case #									
4										
5	DATE	CLIENT	SOURCE OF DEPOSIT	PAYEE	CK #	PURPOSE	CHECKS (SUBTRACT)	DEPOSITS (ADD)	RUNNING BALANCE	MEMO
6	9/10/2012	Student Name				Beginning Balance			$ -	
7	11/14/2012	Student Name		US Mail	3164	Send Filing Packet	$ 10.50		$ (10.50)	
8	1/7/2013	Student Name	Ins. Co	Atty.		Settlement Proceeds		$ 10,000.00	$ 9,989.50	Check No. 1538603
9	1/15/2013	Student Name		Atty.	3201	Fee (25%)	$ 2,500.00		$ 7,489.50	
10	1/15/2013	Student Name		Client	3202	Balance Due Client	$ 7,489.50		$ -	

FIGURE 4.1

f. Apply **General format** to the data in columns B and C and **Accounting Number Format** to the data in columns H, I, and J on the Trust Ledger worksheet.

Apply Additional Formatting to the Trust Ledger

Freeze the panes so that the column headers and dates always remain on-screen and filter the data to show deposits.

a. Select the range **A11:L37** on the Trust Ledger worksheet and format it as a table. Apply the **Table Style Light 1 table style**.

b. Freeze the panes of the chart above and to the left of cell B12 so you can scroll down to the 100 rows you expect to have by the next accounting period.

c. Hide the Purpose column (F) because it is not relevant to the trust ledger.

d. Filter the Payment Received column to show only entries that have contents greater than zero. Four entries should remain.

Insert a Chart of Payments and Charges

For the convenience of your attorney, insert a chart showing the payments received and the payments made (Charges and Administrative Fees) for the trust account.

a. Select the column titles for columns H, I, and J in the Trust Ledger worksheet. Use CTRL to select the **range H37:J37**.

b. Create a bar chart of type **3-D Clustered Bar**.

c. Move the chart and place the top left corner on **cell D40**.

d. Size the chart to a width of **7"** and height of **4.5"**.

e. Select the chart style of your choice.

f. Apply the **Layout 2 chart layout** and remove the axes title.

g. Modify the data labels to font size **12 pt** and drag them to the right so that the full value of the data label is visible.

h. Insert the following two-line title using Shift+Enter to start the second line:

> **Trust Account, Your Name, P.C.**
>
> **Payments and Charges July–December 2013**

i. Change the title font color to **Blue, Accent 1** and deselect the chart.

Print the Trust Ledger

Provide a printed copy of the trust ledger for your attorney and the accountant.

a. Change the scale until the entire Trust Ledger fits on one page width.

b. Hide the gridlines on the Trust Ledger worksheet.

c. Create a footer with this information at the left, center, and right tabs: **Trust Ledger, Confidential, Page 1**.

d. Check the final version using Print Preview.

e. Save and close the workbook. Exit the program and submit based on your instructor's directions.

Use Microsoft Access

Background

Much of the information used by attorneys in their offices can be tracked in a database. It is becoming more common to purchase an integrated case management software program to do this tracking, but many opportunities still exist for a paralegal to make good use of a Microsoft Access database. An Access database can be used to track every part of the law office operation, particularly in a small office that might not have purchased the larger programs due to cost. Even if an Access database is not used, the information in Chapters 1–4 will enhance one's ability to use third-party database programs more effectively.

Tasks

In a small office, a paralegal might be responsible for using Access to prepare the following:

- Client and case tracking
- Contact database, including courts and attorneys
- Trial preparation database (exhibits, documents, etc.)
- Statistical reports

Skills

In addition to basic data entry skills, a paralegal should be able to do the following:

Chapter 1

- Navigate among the objects in an Access database
- Add and edit records
- Back up, compact, and repair Access files
- Sort table data on one or more fields
- Use and remove a filter
- Understand relational power
- Use the Relationships window
- Enforce referential integrity
- Create a database

Chapter 2

- Design a table
- Create and modify tables
- Understand table relationships
- Import and Excel spreadsheet
- Establish table relationships
- Create a single-table query
- Use query design view
- Specify criteria in a query for different data types
- Run, copy, and modify a query
- Create a multitable query
- Modify a multitable query

Chapter 3

- Create a calculated field in a query
- Format and save calculated results
- Verify calculated results
- Create expressions with the Expression Builder
- Use built-in functions in Access
- Create a totals query with grouping

Chapter 4

- Create forms using form tools
- Modify a form
- Revise forms using Layout view
- Identify control types in forms
- Create reports using the Report Wizard
- Modify a report
- Revise reports using Layout and Design views
- Identify control types in reports

Capstone Exercises

As a paralegal for a local law firm, you will be responsible for creating the firm's database and entering data, as well as creating queries, forms, and reports. The database will contain a main table named the Case table and several other supporting tables named CaseType table, County table, and Court table. You will also import the data from several Excel worksheets; the firm has been keeping case data on these worksheets.

Create the Database

Many excellent templates are available in Access, but you decide to create a new blank database for the law firm.

a. Create a blank database and save it as **04a_LawFirm_LastFirst**.

Create the Case Type Table

The attorneys practice primarily family law and handle some criminal law cases. The firm would like to track statistics regarding case type. You need to create a table that stores the case type options.

a. Create a new table named **CaseType**.

b. Create a CaseTypeID field with data type of **AutoNumber**. This field will function as the primary key.

c. Add a second field named **CaseTypeDesc**. It will have a data type of **Short Text** and field size of **25**.

d. Enter the following case types into the table: **Consultation**, **Separation**, **Domestic Violence**, **Divorce**, **Alimony**, **Custody**, **Child Support**, **Parenting Time**, **Paternity**, **Property Settlement**, **Misdemeanor**, **Felony**, and **Other**. On completion of data entry you will have 13 records in the CaseType table.

Create the County Table

The attorneys practice in several counties. Create another table listing the counties in which the attorneys practice.

a. Create a new table named **County**.

b. Create a field named **CountyID** that will function as the primary key, with **AutoNumber** as the Data Type for this field.

c. Add a second field named **CountyDesc**. It will have a Data Type of **Short Text** and field size of **25**.

d. Enter the following four counties into the table: **Genesee**, **Lapeer**, **Shiawassee**, and **Oakland**.

Create the Court Table

The attorneys try cases in multiple jurisdictions: federal, state (civil and criminal courts), and municipal courts. Cases are tried in civil, criminal, appeals, and the Supreme Courts at each level. Create a table listing the courts in which your attorney tries cases.

a. Create a new table named **Court**.

b. Create a field named **CourtID** that will function as the primary key. **AutoNumber** is the Data Type for this field.

c. Add a second field named **CourtDesc**. It will have a Data Type of **Short Text** and field size of **25**.

d. Enter the following four courts into the table: **Civil**, **Criminal**, **Appeals**, and **Supreme**.

Create the Case Table

The main table is the Case table. As you create the fields for this table, you will create the field names that will link to the other three tables.

a. Create a new table named **Case**.

b. Type the field names and data types as indicated in Figure 4.2. Set CaseID as the primary key.

c. Set the following field sizes:

- CaseNo: **15**
- ClientLastName: **25**
- ClientFirstName: **20**

d. Add captions as needed (example: OpenDate should display as Open Date).

e. Save and close the table.

Create and Enforce Relationships

Before entering data into the Case table, create relationships between the tables and enforce referential integrity.

a. Close any open tables.

b. Open the Relationships window. Add the four tables to the Relationships window.

c. Create a relationship between the CaseType table and the Case table using the CaseTypeID field; enforce referential integrity.

d. Create a second relationship between the Court table and the Case table; enforce referential integrity.

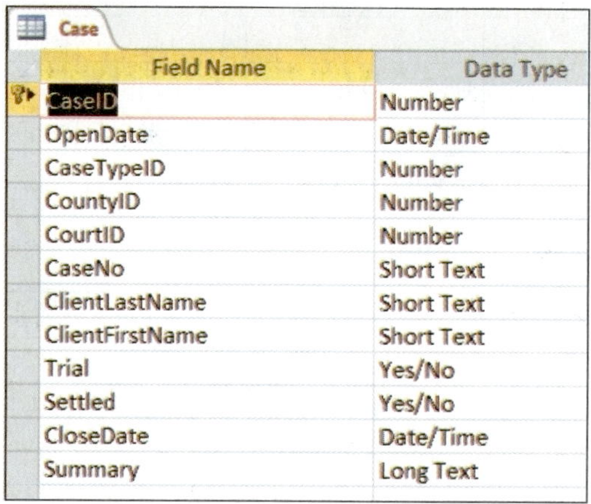

Field Name	Data Type
CaseID	Number
OpenDate	Date/Time
CaseTypeID	Number
CountyID	Number
CourtID	Number
CaseNo	Short Text
ClientLastName	Short Text
ClientFirstName	Short Text
Trial	Yes/No
Settled	Yes/No
CloseDate	Date/Time
Summary	Long Text

FIGURE 4.2

e. Create a third relationship between the County table and the Case table; enforce referential integrity.

f. Place the Case table on the left side of the Relationships window and the other three tables on the right. This will help users to easily interpret the three relationships.

g. Save and close the Relationships window.

Import Excel Records into the Case Table

The law firm used to store cases in an Excel worksheet. Import these records into the Case table.

a. Import external data from the Excel workbook *04a_ImportCases*. Append a copy of the records to the Case table. Use only information from the Sheet1 worksheet with column headings being used as field names for the table.

b. Open the Case table and replace Patricia Larkin's last name and first name with your last name and first name.

c. Filter the records for Case Type 12. Use the Report Wizard to create a report and show the fields CaseTypeID, CaseID, ClientsLastName, and ClientsFirstName, in this specified order. Name the report **CaseTypeID-12 Report**. Close the report. Remove the filter from the table.

d. Sort the records (from A to Z) by Client's Last Name. Remove the sort.

e. Save and close the table.

Enter Case Data Using a Form

Create a simple form using the Form tool and enter the data as shown in the following section.

a. Create a form based on the Case table. Save the form as **Enter Case Data**.

b. Switch to Layout view, if necessary.

c. Change the title label to **Enter and Update Case Data**.

d. Reduce the text box widths to one-half of their original size.

e. Change the form's control padding to **Narrow**.

f. Switch to Form view. Enter the following two new case records:

CaseID	10123	10124
OpenDate	April 1, 2014	March 18, 2014
CaseTypeID	4	12
CountyID	1	3
CourtID	1	4
CaseNo	08-499571	09-203381
ClientLastName	Jimenez	Deheer
ClientFirstName	Jaime	William
Trial	No	No
Settled	Yes	Yes
CloseDate		
Summary	Divorce, 1 child	Possession

g. Close the form.

Create a Single-Table Query

You cannot remember a client's first name, so you create a query to find all clients with the last name Smith.

a. Create a query in Design view and include all fields in the Case table.

b. Add criteria to show all clients with the last name *Smith*.

c. Run the query; three records are displayed.

d. Save the query as **Smith Cases**. Close the query.

Create a Multi-Table Query

Create a query that displays all cases for Genesee County using the CountyID number.

a. Create a query in Design view; include the Case, County, and CaseType tables.

b. Add the CaseID, OpenDate, CloseDate, CaseNo, ClientLastName, and ClientFirstName fields from the Case table, the CaseTypeDesc field from the CaseType table, and the CountyDesc and CountyID fields from the County table.

c. Add criteria to the CountyID field to show only cases for Genesee County and run the query; seven records are displayed.

d. Modify the query to not show the CountyID field in the results. Run the query.

e. Save the query as **Genesee County Cases**. Close the query.

Copy and Modify a Query

Now that you have a query for Genesee County Cases, copy it and paste it using the name **Shiawassee County Cases**.

a. Copy the Genesee County Cases query and paste the query using the name **Shiawassee County Cases**.

b. Modify the CountyID field to locate the Shiawassee cases.

c. Run the query; four records display. Save and close the query.

Calculate Case Duration

The attorneys want to know approximately how long it takes to complete each case. Use the DateDiff() function to calculate the number of days.

a. Create a query using the Case table, the Court table, and the CaseType table.

b. Add the following fields: **CourtDesc, CaseTypeDesc, CaseNo, ClientLastName,** and **ClientFirstName**.

c. Use the Expression Builder to create a field called **DurationDays**; this field should calculate the number of days from the date opened to the date closed using the DateDiff() function.

d. Sort in ascending order by **DurationDays**. Run the query.

e. Clear the Show check box for this field in the query design. Modify the query to only include cases that have a close date. Run the query; 12 records are displayed.

f. Save the query as **Case Duration**. Close the query.

Create a Totals Query

The attorneys want to know the average number of days it takes to complete each type of case.

a. Create a query using the Case table and the CaseType table.

b. Add the fields **CaseTypeDesc** and **CaseID**.

c. Copy the calculated DurationDays field from the Case Duration query, paste the field into the third column, and then change the field name to **AvgDurationDays**.

d. Add the **CloseDate field** in the fourth column.

e. Display the Total row. Group by CaseTypeDesc, count the number of cases, and then calculate the average duration for each type of case. Only include cases with a close date.

f. Run the query and check it for accuracy. (Starting at the top, the Avg Duration by case type should read 136, 341.4, 928, 195, 167, 106, and 119.)

g. Save the query with the name **Avg Duration by Case Type**. Close the query.

Create a Report Using the Report Wizard

The attorneys want you to create a report that lists cases by case type. You decide to create a query first and then use the Report Wizard based on the query.

a. Create a query based on all four tables; add all the fields in the Case table except Trial, Settled, and Summary.

b. Replace the three ID fields with the corresponding Desc field in the related tables.

c. Run the query and examine the results. Save the query as **All Cases**. Close the query.

d. Create a report using the Report Wizard based on the All Cases query.

e. Include all the fields.

f. View by Case and group by CaseTypeDesc.

g. Sort by OpenDate. Choose **landscape**.

h. Name the report **All Cases by Case Type**.

i. Switch to Layout view and adjust the width of the columns so that all data is visible.

j. Switch to Design view, add a CaseTypeDesc footer, and then add a text box control to the CaseID footer. Name the label **Total Cases** and type **=count(*)** in the text box. Display the report in Print Preview mode to test the new control. Align the new total control as needed.

Compact, Repair, and Back Up the Database

An Access database needs to be maintained regularly. It is a good idea to compact, repair, and back up the database each day.

a. Compact and repair the database.

b. Back up the database in the location where you save your student files. When naming the file, include today's date. Close the database and exit the program.

c. Submit the database according to your instructor's directions.

Use Microsoft PowerPoint

Background

Attorneys have historically focused on presenting their information by speaking or writing, and paralegals and legal assistants have aided the attorneys in the preparation for those tasks. Now, technology not only provides paralegals and legal assistants with highly effective tools for researching and document preparation, it has opened the doors to the use of multimedia as a tool for education and in the courtroom. Microsoft PowerPoint is a common tool used in trial openings and closings and as a supplement to a formal presentation. This capstone exercise uses PowerPoint to educate potential clients within a law office. A paralegal or legal assistant would most likely be the person to prepare any kind of PowerPoint supplement that the attorney might want to use.

Tasks

In a small office, the paralegal may be responsible for using PowerPoint to prepare the following:

- Trial exhibits
- Formal presentation slides for a seminar
- Narrated presentations for clients
- Visual aids for the attorney to use when explaining concepts, in paper or electronic form
- Explanatory booklets for clients to take home for review

Skills

In addition to basic formatting skills, a paralegal should be able to do the following:

Chapter 1

- Plan a presentation
- Use slide layouts
- Create a new presentation
- Add new slides
- Use spell check
- Apply themes
- Insert media objects
- Add a table
- Use transitions and animations
- Run and navigate a slide show

Chapter 2

- Import an outline
- Modify a theme

Chapter 3

- Convert text to a SmartArt diagram
- Modify objects
- Arrange objects

Chapter 4

- Insert a picture
- Transform a picture
- Use the Internet as a resource
- Add video
- Use video tools

PARALEGALS

Capstone Exercises

You have been hired by an attorney in the eastern district of Michigan, a consumer bankruptcy specialist, to prepare a PowerPoint presentation that he can use to explain the basics of bankruptcy to potential new clients. You will import the outline provided to you by the attorney and modify the presentation.

Import an Existing Outline

The basic outline has been sent to you by the attorney's office. You create new slides from the outline.

a. Create a new blank presentation and save it as **04p_Bankruptcy_ LastFirst**.

b. Create a handout header with your name and a handout footer with your instructor's name and your class. Include the current date.

c. Create new slides inserting the outline from *04p_Outline.rtf*.

d. Confirm that there is one slide for each major heading element, for a total of 16 slides, including the blank title slide at the beginning of the presentation.

e. Check the presentation for spelling errors and make corrections where needed.

f. View the slide show to familiarize yourself with the content.

Edit the Outline

The outline did not provide a title slide for you, so you must create your own. You edit the outline to create the title slide and edit text. You rearrange and format the slides.

a. Switch to Outline view and enter **Bankruptcy Basics** as the title for Slide 1.

b. Add a two-line subtitle to Slide 1 that reads **Introductory Information for** on the first line, and on the second line, **Clients and Their Family**.

c. Reposition Slide 9 (*Chapter 7 Characteristics*) using the slide sorter so that it becomes Slide 7. Switch to Normal view.

d. On Slide 12, enter **Bekofske's** before *Seven Tests of a Plan* in the **title placeholder** to give credit to Carl Bekofske, the Flint Chapter 13 Trustee who delineated the tests.

e. Change the Bullets format of the text on Slide 12 in the content placeholder to the default Numbering format.

f. On Slide 13, increase the indent level of the bullet *All debtors must personally attend* so that it becomes a subtopic of the first bullet in the list.

g. On Slide 16, convert each of the referenced URLs to hyperlinks.

h. Use the Replace feature to search for the text *Web site:*, (include the colon) and replace it with nothing so that the text does not appear before the hyperlinks you created in the previous step.

Modify the Template

With the text edited, you concentrate on the visual elements of the presentation. You set up the basic theme and color style so you can verify the format of the slides as you work.

a. Apply the **Retrospect design theme**.

b. Apply the **Style 9 background style**.

Modify Title Slide and Create Closing Slide

You modify the title and subtitle of the title slide. You also create a closing slide informing potential clients that there are alternatives to bankruptcy and that they should consult a legal professional. You then add an image and apply a picture style to give the slide dimension.

a. On Slide 1, apply **bold** to the title text.

b. Apply an **Offset Diagonal Bottom Left outer shadow text effect** to the title text.

c. Change the settings of the shadow preset to:

- Transparency: **12%**

- Blur: **6 pt**.

- Angle: **160°**

- Distance: **5 pt**.

d. Change the font size of the subtitle to **16 pt** and apply **Text Shadow**.

e. Create a new slide at the end of the slide show using the *Picture with Caption* layout. Enter **There are alternatives to Bankruptcy** in the **title placeholder**. In the Font dialog box, select the option **All Caps**.

f. Enter **Discuss Options with the Attorney** in the **subtitle placeholder**.

g. Click the icon to insert *04p_LawBooks.jpg* into the picture placeholder. Apply a **Drop Shadow Rectangle picture style**.

Add SmartArt

You add SmartArt diagrams to the presentation to enhance its appearance and to provide the client a break from the bullet format used by the majority of slides. You apply a list SmartArt to the list of bankruptcy types on Slide 6 and a process SmartArt to the duties of Chapter 13 filers on Slide 13.

a. On Slide 6, convert the existing text to a **Vertical Box List SmartArt**.

b. Change the colors of the SmartArt to **Colorful Range–Accent Colors 2 to 3**.

c. Apply the **Moderate Effect style** to the SmartArt.

d. On Slide 13, convert the existing text to a **Step Down Process SmartArt**.

e. Apply the **Moderate Effect style** to the SmartArt.

Insert a Table

It would be useful to show statistics on the number of bankruptcy cases filed in the eastern district of Michigan where the attorney practices law.

a. Create a new slide after Slide 10 using the *Title and Content* layout.

b. Enter a two-line title with **United States Bankruptcy Court** on the first line and **Eastern District of Michigan** on the second line.

c. Insert a six-column by eight-row table.

d. Merge and center the cells in the top row of the table and enter the table heading **201x Bankruptcy Statistics** where x is the year you chose (see step f).

e. Go to the Web site **www.mieb.uscourts.gov/**. Select **Court Info** from the menu bar and select **Court Statistics**.

f. View the current year's statistics from the list at the bottom of the chart. (Note: If the current year does not include statistics for January through June, go to the previous year.)

g. Copy the column headings (*Chapter 7, Chapter 11, Chapter 12, Chapter 13, Totals*) and paste the headings on the table you created in PowerPoint, leaving the first cell blank. Copy all the data for the months January through June and paste the data in the table you created in PowerPoint.

Insert and Modify Images

You decide to insert a bankruptcy-related image and modify it to further enhance the presentation.

a. On Slide 4, insert *04p_Relief.jpg* and change the height of the image to **2.5"**.

b. Drag the image so that it is aligned at the bottom center.

c. Remove the white background from the image so the sign and bar are visible. Nudge the image up above the slide bottom border so that all parts of the image are seen.

Apply Animations and a Transition

a. Select the title placeholder on Slide 2, apply the **Zoom animation**, and then set the animation to start **After Previous**.

b. Select the bullet placeholder on Slide 2 and apply the **Appear animation**. Set the animation effect options to **By Paragraph**, if necessary, and then set the animation to start **After Previous**.

c. Select the image on Slide 4, apply the **Grow & Turn animation**, and then set the animation to start **After Previous**.

d. Select the **bullet placeholder** on Slide 4, apply the **Wipe animation**, set the animation to start **After Previous**, and then set the duration to **2.00**.

e. Select the **SmartArt** on Slide 6, apply the **Fly In animation** with a **From Top effect options** and **As One Object sequence**. Set the animation to start **After Previous** and with a duration of **.75**.

f. Apply the **Uncover transition** to all slides.

g. View the presentation.

h. Save and close **04p_Bankruptcy_LastFirst**. Exit the program and submit based on your instructor's directions.

Integrate Microsoft Office Programs

Background

In addition to working with individual Microsoft Office applications and legal management software, efficient paralegals and legal assistants often integrate content that has been created in different applications to complete projects.

Tasks

Microsoft Word is frequently the host program when integrating content created in other applications. Microsoft PowerPoint is often the host for training material and is used for trial introductions and exhibits. Both Microsoft Excel and Microsoft Access are good programs for storing, organizing, retrieving, and indexing materials. In addition, Excel's ability to create charts from worksheet data could be particularly applicable in tax, probate, real estate, and trial work. Examples of integrated law office tasks that integrate data from multiple programs could include the following:

- Communicate clearly and effectively by creating merge documents in Word that utilize data from an Excel or Access file
- Embed or link Excel worksheets or charts into Word documents or PowerPoint slides
- Create PowerPoint presentations with various linked or embedded objects from Word and Excel

Skills

In addition to skills in each application program, a paralegal should be able to do the following:

- Create and utilize a database containing contact information
- Create a merge source file
- Format a worksheet
- Create a chart in Excel
- Embed and link content from multiple sources
- Choose records or fields to merge
- Create a flyer
- Create a presentation file

PARALEGALS

Capstone Exercises

Donna DeWitt, an attorney in your state, has decided to run for the family court judicial vacancy. Because her legal staff performs specifically delegated tasks in her legal office, she is outsourcing her campaign materials to you, a paralegal. You will prepare many of her promotional materials. You will integrate data from Office programs to produce professional products for her.

Before starting, you make a call to the Genesee County Bar Association to speak with Ms. Ramona Sain, the executive director of the association, for advice on what to include in the publicity announcements. Ms. Sain suggests that you create a database of names of possible supporters, starting with local attorneys. She provides you with a list or supporters as well as the results of a candidate survey. You will send the attorneys a personalized letter announcing Donna's candidacy, outlining her qualifications, and including the results of a survey. She also suggests you prepare a flyer that can be printed and distributed in various sizes, as well as used in the DeWitt for Judge Web site. With those suggestions in mind, you prepare the promotional materials.

Create a Database of Recipient Names

Ms. Sain has provided you with an Excel worksheet that includes the names of attorneys in the area who should be recipients of the letter announcing Donna's candidacy. You import the Excel data into an Access database and create a new form so additional names can be added to the database. Because Donna will be visiting law offices in Flint next week, you query the database for Flint law office data and prepare a report for printing so that Donna has the addresses of the offices she can visit during her trip.

a. Create a new, blank Access database. Name it **04i_Contacts_LastFirst**.

b. Create a table by importing external data from the Excel worksheet *04i_ContactInfo.xlsx*. Complete the Get External Data - Excel Spreadsheet wizard, taking only information from Sheet1. Indicate that the first row contains column headings. All of the fields use the Text data type. Let Access add the primary key. Name the table **Contacts**. Do not save the import steps.

c. Use the Form tool to create a form that can be used to enter or modify records in the Contacts table. Save the form and name it **Contacts Form**.

d. Create a query using the Contacts table. Select the **City**, **Company**, **Address**, **Address2**, **LastName**, and **FirstName fields**.

e. Use *Flint* as the criterion for the City field to limit the output to only law offices located in Flint.

f. Sort the query fields first by Company and then by LastName and FirstName.

g. Save the query as **Flint Law Offices**.

h. Compact and repair the database.

i. Close the Access database and exit the program.

Start the Mail Merge Process and Select the Recipient List

Ms. Sain indicated the first step in the campaign will be to send a letter to attorneys thanking them for their survey ratings and enlisting their support. You format a document that has already been created and which will be the main document in the merge process. You modify the format so that the letter fits on one page, making it possible to mail it in a window envelope. Format the letter now, and in a later exercise you will insert a chart and complete the merge.

a. Open the file *04i_Letter.docx*. Save it as **04i_Letter_LastFirst**.

b. Set the top and bottom margins to **0.5** and set the page vertical alignment to **center**.

c. Enter the following return address at the top of the Word document.

Committee for the Election of Donna DeWitt

PO Box 12345

Flint, MI 48501-1234

d. Apply the **Metropolitan theme** to the document.

e. Apply the **WordArt style 8** to the text *Committee for the Election of Donna DeWitt* in the return address. Set the WordArt text to bold, **16 pt**. Delete the original text and drag the WordArt above the post office box line. Center the WordArt and press **Enter** to insert a blank line.

f. Add a tab stop behind the zip code to right align the e-mail address, which is donnadewittforjudge@yahoo.com. Enter a blank space to create the e-mail address hyperlink and press **Enter** twice.

g. Insert the date in the Month Day, Year format. Do not update automatically. Press **Enter** twice to insert a blank line after the date.

h. Start the mail merge by using the Step-by-Step Mail Merge Wizard to select the Letters mail merge process.

i. Use the current document to start the letter.

j. Select recipients from the Contacts table stored in the *04i_Contacts_LastFirst* database. Refine the recipient list using the LastName field by sorting it in ascending order.

k. Insert an Address block using the default form of *Joshua Randall Jr.* as the recipient name. Be sure to include the three other default choices: *Insert company name*, *Insert postal address*, and *Format address according to the destination country/region*.

l. Press **Enter** twice to insert a blank line and add a subject line with **RE: Peer Candidate Ratings**.

m. Press **Enter** twice to insert a blank line and create a greeting line that will insert the greeting line fields in the format of

Dear Joshua Randall, Jr.,. Press **Enter** twice to insert a blank line after the greeting line.

n. You are on Step 4 of the Mail Merge Wizard. Save the document and minimize the program window so you can later return to complete the merge process.

Format the Approval Rating Worksheet

Ms. Sain provided you with an Excel workbook displaying the approval rating statistics for Donna compiled from a survey of attorneys. Format the worksheet and prepare a chart depicting her ratings.

a. Open the Excel workbook *04i_Responses.xlsx* and save as **04i_Responses_LastFirst**.

b. Apply the **Metropolitan theme** to the worksheet.

c. Merge and center the *Opinion Responses: Donna DeWitt* title across columns A–I. Apply the **Accent4 style** to the resulting cell. Bold the selected title and increase the font size to **16 pt**.

d. Apply the **20% – Accent4 style** to cell **A3** (Summary Statistics). Bold the text.

e. Select the **range A3:C5** and apply the **Outside Borders border style**.

f. Format the **range A7:I7** as **Text** and center the text.

g. Format the **range A7:H142** as a table and apply the **Table Style Medium 19 style**.

h. Change the column width of columns A to I to **14 pt**.

i. Wrap the text in the column headings.

j. Proofread the column headings and edit the text so that the headings use consistent capitalization.

k. Remove the filter arrows from the column headings.

Insert Basic Statistical Functions into the Approval Rating Worksheet

With the formatting in place, add basic statistical functions to the worksheet. Calculate the number of responses to the survey, the average by question and average by person, and a final average score for the candidate. The final average score will be published in the promotional materials.

a. Add a new column heading **Average Rating by Person** in **cell I7**.

b. Insert a formula that computes the average rating by person in **cell I8** to compute the rating for each respondent in the survey. Display the results to one decimal place. (Note: If Excel prompts you that adjacent cells are not part of the formula, ignore the error. Column A is the Respondent # and should not be included in the calculations.)

c. Add a Total Row to the table and change *Total* to **Average**. Calculate the average for each column displaying the results to one decimal place.

d. Turn on Banded Columns.

e. Enter the number of responses to the survey in **cell C4** using the appropriate function to count the responses.

f. Calculate the Final Average Score in **cell C5** using the information in column I and display to one decimal place.

g. Remove the filter arrow from the new column heading.

Create a Chart of Approval Ratings

A visual depiction of the approval ratings will help most people quickly understand the ratings. Use the average ratings for each characteristic to format a chart for inclusion on promotional materials.

a. Select the column headings in rows B through H and the average for each characteristic.

b. Insert a clustered 2-D Clustered Bar chart.

c. Resize the chart to **3"** high by **6"** wide and center the chart below the worksheet.

d. Change the chart layout to **Layout 1**.

e. Apply **Chart Style 3**.

f. Change the chart title to **Donna DeWitt, Peer Approval Ratings**.

g. Change the chart title font to **20 pt**, if necessary.

h. Switch the Row/Column data to display the characteristics on the vertical axis and the series in the legend.

i. Remove the legend.

j. Add a primary horizontal axis title that reads **Average Points, Scale of 1–9**.

k. Remove the display of the primary horizontal axis and save the *04i_Responses_LastFirst* workbook. Do not close the workbook until after the next series of steps where the chart is linked to the letter.

Insert the Chart into the Letter

Copy the chart and paste it into the prepared letter.

a. Copy the chart you created in the *04i_Responses_LastFirst* workbook. Save the workbook and close Excel.

b. Maximize the Word file *04i_Letter_LastFirst* from the taskbar, as it was minimized earlier.

c. Place the insertion point at the end of the sentence behind the text *The results are summarized below:*

d. Use Paste with the option to **Keep Source Formatting & Link Data** to embed and link the chart.

e. Set the text to **wrap top and bottom**. There should be a blank line after the chart before the next paragraph.

f. Change the chart's width to **5.2"** and the height to **2.2"** and **center align** the chart.

Completing the Merge

After completing the main document and the data source file, you are ready to complete the merge process.

a. Finish and merge the main document and the data source file. **Do not** print the documents. (There will be 60 letters.)

b. Your final letter should look like Figure 4.3.

c. Save the merged letter file as **04i_Merge_LastFirst** and close the document.

d. Save **04i_Letter_LastFirst** and close the document.

e. Exit both programs Word and Excel. Submit files as directed by your instructor.

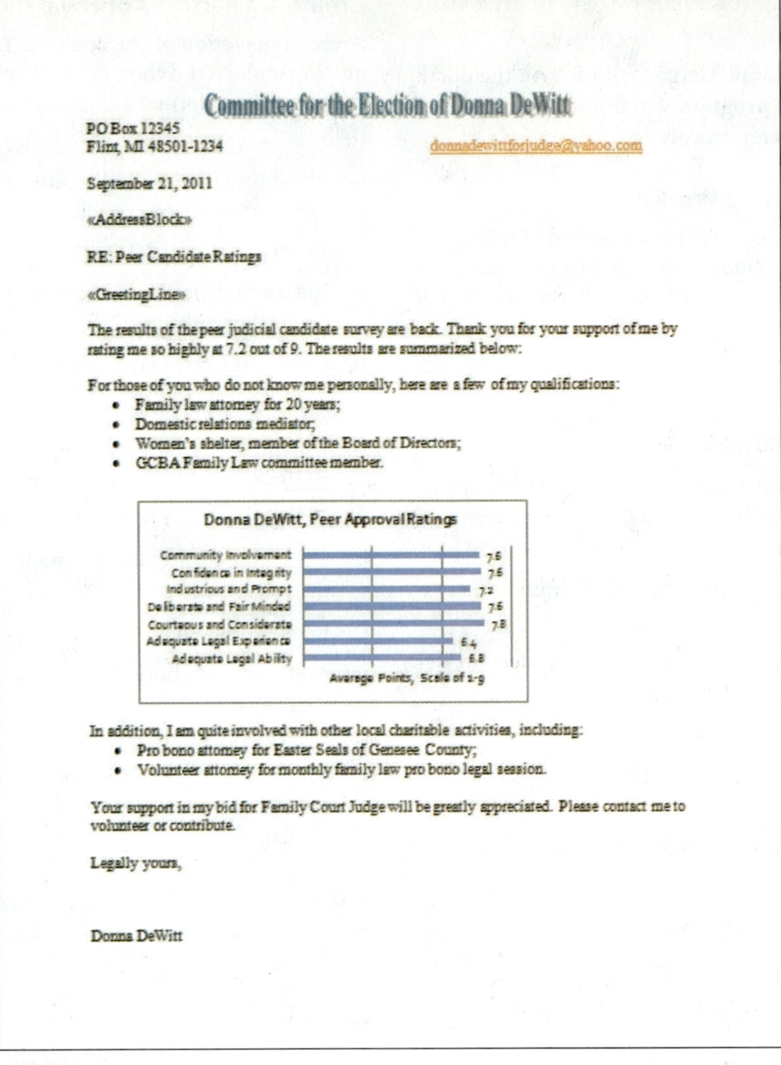

FIGURE 4.3

Create a Flyer in PowerPoint

You need a simple but attractive flyer that can be distributed around the city. It should outline the attorney's major qualifications.

a. Open a new PowerPoint presentation. Save it as **04i_Flyer_LastFirst**.

b. Change the layout of Slide 1 to **Title Only** and change the slide size for Letter Paper with **Portrait orientation**. Select the option to maximize the size of your content to fit on the new slide.

c. Select the **Parallax theme**.

d. Set the background to **Background Style 1**.

e. Create the following two-line main title:

Donna DeWitt

for Family Court Judge

f. Select the two-line title and change the font color to **Blue** and the font to **Calibri**.

g. Select the **title placeholder** and apply a Shape Style of **Subtle Effect – Blue, Accent 1**. Resize the title placeholder to a height of **2"**.

h. Select the text *Donna DeWitt* and increase the font size until the text fills the width of the title placeholder.

i. Select the *for Family Court Judge* text and change the font size until the text is approximately as wide as the line *Donna DeWitt* above but does not extend below the placeholder border.

j. Select both lines of text and apply a Glow shape effect of **Blue, 11 pt glow, Accent color 1**.

k. Insert the image *04i_Dewitt.tif* below the title placeholder and resize the image to a height of **3.5"** and a width of **2.85"**. Increase the brightness of the image 15%. Flip the image horizontally. Position the image horizontally at **0.8"** and vertically **2.7"** from the top left corner.

l. Insert a Varying Width List SmartArt and add the text below:

• **Family Law Attorney, 10 years**

• **Domestic Relations Mediator**

• **Women's Shelter, Board of Directors**

m. Resize the SmartArt and reposition it so that the right edge of the SmartArt aligns with the right edge of the title placeholder and the top of the SmartArt is aligned with the DeWitt image. (Do not allow SmartArt to cover any portion of the image.)

FIGURE 4.4

n. Apply the **Subtle Effect SmartArt style**.

o. Open the Excel file *04i_Responses_LastFirst* and copy the Donna DeWitt, Peer Approval Ratings chart. Do not close the program until step q is done.

p. Use Paste with the option to Keep Source Formatting & Link Data to embed and link the chart on the slide below the picture.

q. Change the chart height to **2.7"** and the width to **5.4"**. The chart should not overlap the graphic background on the left.

r. Close the Excel program and if prompted to save the file, do not save the file; no changes should have been made to the workbook.

s. Insert a text box at the bottom right of the flyer. Enter the following text:

Committee for the Election of Donna DeWitt

donnadewittforjudge@yahoo.com

t. Change the font size to **10 pt**.

u. Adjust the size of any of the images to appear similar to what is given. The final flyer should look like Figure 4.4.

v. Save **04i_Flyer_LastFirst** and close the document. Submit according to the directions of your instructor.

Create a Running PowerPoint Slide Show

Donna DeWitt is planning to have an election table at the Genesee County Fair. She asked you to create a short PowerPoint slide presentation to run automatically at the fair. Because of the noisy, outdoor environment you do not use sound, but you insert animation on each slide to catch the attention of people passing the election table. Use the PowerPoint flyer and reconfigure it to run as a short kiosk presentation.

a. Open *04i_Flyer_LastFirst* and save it as **04i_Fair_LastFirst**.

b. Customize the slide size by changing the orientation to **Landscape** using the option Ensure Fit to scale it down to ensure it will fit on the new slide.

FIGURE 4.5

c. Make three duplicates of the existing slide to now have four slides.

d. On Slide 1, change the layout to the **Title Only slide layout**. Delete the SmartArt, the chart, and the text box. Change the title placeholder to a height of **1.8"** and a width of **7.5"**.

e. Apply Reset to the image size and Reset to the picture corrections so the image is returned to original state. Apply the **Center Shadow Rectangle picture style** to the image. Arrange the title placeholder and the picture attractively on the slide.

f. Apply the **Shape animation** to Donna DeWitt's image and modify the effect options so that the direction is **Out** and the shape is **Box**. Set the animation to **After Previous**.

g. On Slide 2, change the layout to the **Blank layout**. Delete the chart, the photograph, and the text box.

h. Edit the title placeholder text to: **Qualifications**. Change the width to **7.5"** and apply **Align Center**.

i. Change the SmartArt layout to **Vertical Box List**. Change the width to **7.5"** and apply **align center**. Select the alignment option to **distribute vertically** and put space between the title placeholder and the SmartArt.

j. Animate the SmartArt so each line **Fades In** one by one **after the previous** animation. Set the delay to **01.50 seconds**.

k. On Slide 3, change the layout to the **Blank layout** and remove all but the title placeholder and the chart.

l. Change the title placeholder text to **Peer Approval Ratings**. Change the width to **7.5"** and apply **align center**.

m. Change the chart height to **4.3"** and width to **7.5"**.

n. Remove the chart title.

o. Position the chart attractively on the slide while ensuring that it does not overlap the slide design elements.

p. Animate the chart so category information **Wipes** from the left by the elements in the category. Set the animation to start **After Previous**. Set the delay to **0.50 seconds**.

q. On Slide 4, change the layout to **Title slide layout**. Delete the SmartArt, the chart, the picture, and the subtitle placeholder. Replace the title placeholder text with the following text:

Vote for

Donna DeWitt

Family Court Judge

November 6th

r. Format the text of the first two lines to font size **60 pt** and the other two lines as **36 pt**. Resize the shape to fit the text, if necessary.

s. Change the placeholder's shape style to **Colored Outline – Blue, Accent 1**. Change the width to **8.5"** and apply **Align Middle** to the placeholder. Remove the lines from the outside of the placeholder.

t. Resize all of the text in the *Committee for the Election of Donna DeWitt* box to **18 pt**. Change the width to **5.0"**. Apply **align bottom** and **align right** to the text box.

u. Apply the **Zoom entrance animation** to the title placeholder and set it to animate **After Previous**.

v. Apply the **Flip transition** to all slides and advance slides automatically after **6 seconds**.

w. Set up the slide show to be **browsed at a kiosk** using automatic timings.

x. View the presentation.

y. Adjust any image or placeholder position so the final slides look like Figure 4.5.

z. Save the presentation and exit the program. Submit according to the directions of your instructor.

Science Discipline

Using Microsoft Office as a Science Professional

BACKGROUND | Working as a Science Professional

There are many different branches of science, including chemistry, biology, physics, earth and space sciences, environmental sciences, and the behavioral and social sciences. Given the technological advances in science and research, a career in science requires a certain level of expertise in computer competency, including a familiarity with a variety of software applications.

Strong organization skills are paramount for anyone working in science, especially while collecting and recording the results of experiments or compiling research for reports and papers. You also need to keep samples and research organized and accessible. In addition, the ability to analyze and draw conclusions from gathered data is essential. An Access database is an exceptional tool for organizing, storing, and manipulating data. Scientists also use Excel spreadsheets to compute and analyze data in tables as well as to illustrate trends and make comparisons with charts and graphs.

In addition to organization skills, scientists are required to use word-processing software such as Word to write reports and integrate data and graphs into these reports to communicate their findings or observations. Moreover, scientists may be required to use presentation software such as PowerPoint to convey the results of their studies to an audience.

Using Office in Science

Application	Exercises	Skills Covered
1. WORD Data Files: 05w_Report Solution Files: 05w_Report_Solution	LAB REPORT (page 97)	• Review Word usage in a document • Insert headers and footers • Insert a symbol • Adjust margins • View a document and manage page flow • Customize document properties • Select font options • Change text appearance • Use and modify styles • Select paragraph alignment • Select line and paragraph spacing • Create bulleted and numbered lists • Insert a textbox • Format text into columns • Create or draw a table • Insert and delete rows and columns • Merge cells • Change row height and column width • Adjust table position and alignment • Format table text • Use a formula • Convert text to table • Add a comment • View and reply to comments • Use Track changes • Accept and reject changes • Create a source • Create a footnote
2. EXCEL Data Files: 05e_FermentationLab Solution Files: 05e_DensityLab_Solution 05e_FermentationLab_Solution	LAB EXPERIMENTS (page 100)	• Enter text • Enter values • Enter formulas • Copy formulas using AutoFill • Rename a worksheet • Manage columns and rows • Apply alignment and font options • Apply number formats • Select page setup options • Use cell references in formulas • Use the average function • Insert statistical functions • Determine results with the IF function • Use lookup functions • Create a range name • Use a range name in a formula • Select the data source • Move, size and print a chart • Create a line chart • Create an XY (Scatter) chart • Move a chart • Add chart elements • Format chart elements • Create a table • Add and delete fields • Apply a table style • Sort data • Filter data • Use structured references • Apply conditional formatting • Create a new rule
3. ACCESS Data Files: 05a_GroveCreek 05a_CreekSampleResults.xlsx Solution Files: 05a_GroveCreek_Solution	WATER SAMPLE DATABASE (page 104)	• Add, edit and delete records • Compact the database • Sort table data • Create, modify and remove filters • Understand relational power • Create and modify a table • Share data • Establish table relationships • Create a single-table query • Specify query criteria for different data types • Understand query sort order • Run, copy, and modify a query • Create a multi-table query • Modify a multi-table query • Create calculated field in a query • Format and save calculated results • Use built in functions in Access • Add aggregate functions to datasheets • Create queries with aggregate functions • Create forms using form tools • Use form views • Sort records in a form • Create reports using report tools • Use report views • Modify a report • Apply conditional formatting

| 4. POWERPOINT
Data Files: 05p_Writing
05p_Scientist.jpg
05_Music.mid

Solution Files:
05p_Guidelines_Solution | WRITING GUIDE PRESENTATION
(page 108) | • Use PowerPoint views • Insert media objects • Add a table • Use animations and transitions • Insert a header and footer • Run and navigate a slideshow • Modify an outline structure • Reuse slides from an existing presentation • Use sections • Modify a theme • Modify a slide master • Create shapes • Apply Quick Styles and customize shapes • Create SmartArt • Modify SmartArt • Create WordArt • Modify WordArt • Insert a picture • Transform a picture • Add audio • Change audio settings |
| 5. INTEGRATED
Data Files: 05i_Survey.accdb
05i_SpringResults.accdb
05i_SurveyAddresses.xlsx
05i_WeightChange.docx
05i_Thankyou.docx

Solution Files:
05i_Survey_Solution.accdb
05i_SurveyStatistics_Solution.xlsx
05i_WeightChange_Solution.docx
05i_Merged_Solution.docx
05i_Thankyou_Solution.docx | RESEARCH PROJECT
(page 111) | • Create graphs and charts from Excel data • Paste Excel worksheets or charts into a Word document • Import data from Excel into Access • Create queries with calculated fields • Create a report in Access • Format a document • Use Mail Merge |

Use Microsoft Word

Background

College students majoring in the sciences will often be required to write formal reports. Knowing how to create, format, review, and make changes to documents are necessary skills. It is important that students understand the features of Microsoft Word that are available in order to create an effective scientific document.

Tasks

Scientific research, whether it be from experiments performed or literature reviewed, requires some kind of documents to be created. Such documents could include the following:

- Lab reports
- Scientific papers
- Research papers
- Abstracts
- Correspondence

Skills

In addition to basic formatting skills, students writing a variety of scientific documents should be able to do the following:

Chapter 1

- Review Word usage in a document
- Insert headers and footers
- Insert a symbol
- Adjust margins
- View a document and manage page flow
- Customize document properties

Chapter 2

- Select font options
- Change text appearance
- Use and modify styles
- Select paragraph alignment
- Select line and paragraph spacing
- Create bulleted and numbered lists
- Insert a textbox
- Format text into columns

Chapter 3

- Create or draw a table
- Insert and delete rows and columns
- Merge cells
- Change row height and column width
- Adjust table position and alignment
- Format table text
- Use a formula
- Convert text to table

Chapter 4

- Add a comment
- View and reply to comments
- Use Track changes
- Accept and reject changes
- Create a source
- Create a footnote

Capstone Exercises

You are a student taking an introductory chemistry course. You are required to write a formal, typed laboratory report in conjunction with the experiment you and your lab partner just completed. You wrote up the preliminary report and asked your partner to review it and make corrections or additions. You now need to add the data tables and format it according to the instructor's specifications before you submit it to the professor.

Track Revisions

Your lab partner has reviewed the initial lab report and has made some changes, and inserted some comments. You need to review the document comments and accept or reject the revisions before you add additional content.

a. Open *05w_Report.docx* and save it as **05w_Report_LastFirst**.

b. Ensure that the markup view is *All Markup* on the Review tab, in the Tracking group. With the insertion point at the top of the page, use the Next Change button in the Changes group to move to the last sentence in paragraph one that has to do with the accuracy of this experiment (*If you are not careful….*). Click Reject to discard the insertion of this sentence.

c. Accept the insertion of the sentence in the next paragraph that begins with (*Let the solution cool…*).

d. Reply to the comment by typing, **I will add the conclusions we mentioned yesterday.**

e. Turn off the Tracking feature on the Review tab, change the markup view to No Markup, and then move to the beginning of the document.

Format the Document

The instructor has distributed the formatting specifications. Apply the following formatting features to meet the requirements for the paper.

a. Add your name after *Name:*, your instructor's name after *Lab Partner*, and the current date.

b. Set the left and right margins to 1".

c. Insert a page number at the bottom of the page using the **Bold Numbers 3**.

d. Select the entire document and change the font to **Times New Roman**, font size **12 pt**.

e. Center align the title of the document and change the font size to **14 pt**.

f. Right align the information above the title of the paper beginning with *Name* and ending with *Date*. Change the line spacing to single.

g. Apply the **Subtitle** style to all of the headings (*Abstract, Introduction, Materials, Procedure, Results, References,* and *Conclusion*).

h. Modify the Subtitle style to font size **12 pt** and **Italic**.

Format the Materials Section

The list in the Materials section needs to be formatted as a bulleted list and needs a text box added for additional information.

a. Select the list of materials and convert it to a bulleted list.

b. Format the list to two columns.

c. Draw a text box after the list of materials and type **Dilution Equation ($M_1V_1 = M_2V_2$)**.

d. Format the text in the text box to Times New Roman, font size **12 pt**, No Outline, and change the height of the textbox to **0.3"** and the width to **2.45"**.

e. Change the text wrapping to Square and center align the textbox.

Create a New Table

You need to add a table to the Procedure section of the report.

a. Insert a blank line after the first paragraph in the Procedure section.

b. Create a table with five columns and six rows.

c. Merge the cells of the first row and type the following: **Preparation of Standards Solutions**.

d. Enter the following headings and data:

Solution	mL Stock Iron Solution	Drops of Citrate	mL Hydroquinone	mL Phenanthroline
1	1	6	1	1.5
2	2	12	1	1.5
3	3	18	1	1.5
4	5	30	1	1.5

e. Insert a row below the headings, type **Blank** as the *Solution* type, and then complete the rest of the row with the following data:

Blank	0	0	0	1.5

f. Change the line spacing of row 2 to Single, with no spacing after.

g. Change the height of row 2 to **0.4**.

h. Format the table using the **Grid Table 1 Light** table style.

i. Center align the contents of the table cells.

j. Add a footnote to the mL Stock Iron Solution heading: **Stock iron solution provided by instructor**.

Use Advanced Table Features

Some of the data from the experiment was entered into a table in the Results section and some of the data was not. It needs to be improved and some calculations need to be performed.

a. In the Results section, insert a new row above the first row in the table to add a title. Type **Table 1: Calibration Curve Data Table**.

b. Merge the cells and top center align the title.

c. Format the table to AutoFit Window and apply the **Grid Table 1 Light** table style.

d. Select the text below the paragraph "Table 2 summarizes the results…" and convert the text to a table with four columns.

e. Insert a new column on the right. Create a formula to average the Absorbance of the Iron Tablet Solution, the Mass of the Fe of Tablet, and the Percent Error.

f. Insert a new row above the first row in the table to add a title. Type **Table 2: Iron Tablet Data**, merge the cells, and then center align the title.

g. Center align the contents of table 2.

h. Format the table using the **Grid Table 1 Light** table style.

Create a Source and Add It to the Document

The instructor created this experiment based on a journal article. You need to create the source, add it to the Reference section, and format it accordingly.

a. Using Manage Sources on the Reference tab, add a new source using the APA style for a journal article: Author: **Atkins, Robert C.**

Title: **Colorimetric Determination of Iron in Vitamin Supplement Tablets: A General Chemistry Experiment**

Journal: **Journal of Chemical Education**

Year: **1975**

Page: **550**

b. Click on the blank line below the Reference section. Click on Bibliography, and select Insert Bibliography to insert the source.

Final Review of the Document

As you proofread the report, you realize you need to make a few more additions and changes to the document.

a. Insert missing text in the third paragraph of the Introduction section. As you begin to review the report, you notice that the formula for Beer's Law is incomplete: *Beer's Law (A = bc)*. Insert the symbol ε (Greek small letter epsilon – 03B5, which can be found in Font – Times New Roman text, Subset – Greek and Coptic), so that the formula reads $A = \varepsilon bc$.

b. Add a few sentences to the conclusion section. Type the following under the Conclusion heading:

The vitamin tablet was tested twice, and the results were in an acceptable percent error range. Miscalculations in this experiment can be traced to the difficulties in measuring the volume in the graduated cylinder and Erlenmeyer flasks. With experience, technical variations may be overcome. Overall, the vitamin tablet tested did come close to the amounts claimed by the manufacturer.

c. Perform a spelling and grammar check of the document. Accept all references to *analyte* as the correct spelling and accept *HCL* and *phenanthroline* as correct spellings.

d. Insert a page break before the Conclusions section.

Change the Document Properties and Save the Document

a. Open the Document Panel and add the keywords: **Iron, Beer's Law, Absorbance**.

b. Save and close the document.

c. Submit the file based on your instructor's directions.

Use Microsoft Excel

Background

College students taking science courses often perform experiments to test a hypothesis. Data is recorded in a lab notebook. Knowing how to use Microsoft Excel to enter and format data, perform calculations, and create graphs and charts is required. It is important that students are proficient in using Microsoft Excel.

Tasks

Almost all scientific experiments need to use worksheets to analyze data and visually interpret those results. Such worksheets could include the following:

- Entering and formatting data
- Analyzing data using formulas and functions
- Creating graphs and charts

Skills

The need to manage, manipulate, and display data using worksheets requires that students should be able to do the following:

Chapter 1

- Enter text
- Enter values
- Enter formulas
- Copy formulas using AutoFill
- Rename a worksheet
- Manage columns and rows
- Apply alignment and font options
- Apply number formats
- Select page setup options

Chapter 2

- Use cell references in formulas
- Use the average function
- Insert statistical functions
- Determine results with the IF function
- Use lookup functions
- Create a range name
- Use a range name in a formula

Chapter 3

- Select the data source
- Move, size, and print a chart
- Create a line chart
- Create an XY (Scatter) chart
- Move a chart
- Add chart elements
- Format chart elements

Chapter 4

- Create a table
- Add and delete fields
- Apply a table style
- Sort data
- Filter data
- Use structured references
- Apply conditional formatting
- Create a new rule

Capstone Exercises

You have a busy semester with your science classes, and all of them expect you to be able to use Excel to report your findings, perform calculations, and create visual representations of the data. You recorded the results of your chemistry experiment in your lab notebook, and now it is time to enter the data into Excel. When you are done entering the data, you will need to create formulas and generate some graphs. For your biology course, you conducted an experiment and created an Excel workbook to record your results. You want to use the table feature to filter and sort the data to analyze the results. You also need to create a chart to visualize one of the categories of your experiment.

Enter and Format the Text Labels

You are ready to create the first Excel worksheet. You have planned the structure of your worksheet and decide to enter all of the labels first and do some basic formatting before you enter the values and create formulas. You make sure that you have placed the data, in this case volume before mass, to make the creation of charts easier.

a. Create a new workbook and save it as **05e_DensityLab_ LastFirst**.

b. Type the worksheet title, **Density Determination of Unknown Metal Sample**, in **cell A1**.

c. Merge and center the range **A1:G1**. Middle Align the merged cell.

d. Apply bold and 16 pt font.

e. Select **row 1** and format the row height to 35.

f. Rename the sheet **Data**.

g. Type the following labels:

- **Sample ID** in **cell A3**
- **Volume (mL)** in **cell B3**
- **Mass (g)** in **cell C3**
- **Density (g/mL)** in **cell D3**
- **Average Density** in **cell A12**
- **Standard Deviation** in **cell A13**
- **Identity of Sample** in **cell A14**

h. Wrap the text in the range **A3:D3**; apply bold; change the fill color to Blue, Accent 1, Lighter 60%; and center align the contents.

i. Select column A and format it using AutoFit Column Width.

Enter the Lab Data

Using the data recorded in your lab notebook, you are ready to enter your results. You were given six metal samples of varying mass, and using the volume displacement method, you need to determine what kind of metal the sample is. You have already calculated the volume of each sample (subtracting the initial water volume from the final water volume).

a. Enter the data into your Data worksheet as shown below:

	A	B	C	D	E	F	G
1	Density Determination of Unknown Metal Sample						
2							
3	Sample ID	Volume (mL)	Mass (g)	Density (g/mL)			
4	1	2.51	6.75				
5	2	3.39	9.7				
6	3	4.59	12.44				
7	4	5.13	13.8				
8	5	5.72	15.44				
9	6	6.87	18.36				
10							

b. Format the **range B4:C9** with the Number format, with two decimals.

c. Select the range **A4:A9** and center the Sample IDs.

Use Formulas and Functions

Now that you have designed your worksheet and entered the data, you are ready to create a formula to determine the density of each sample. You also need to calculate the average density and standard deviations.

a. In **cell D4**, create a formula to determine the density of each sample. Density = Mass/Volume.

b. Copy the formula for the rest of the samples.

c. Enter a function in **cell C12** to calculate the average density of all the samples.

d. In **cell C13**, create a formula to calculate the standard deviation (STDEVA) for the range **D4:D9**.

e. Format the ranges **D4:D9** and **C12:C13** with the Number format.

Use a Lookup Function

You also need to make sure your worksheet contains information for the true density (accepted density) of known metal substances so you can identify your sample. Your instructor has given the list of the class samples and the true density from your chemistry textbook. You will use a lookup function to assign the substance name that corresponds with the average density result.

a. Create a lookup table starting in **cell A16**, using the data shown below. Apply the **Number** format, with two decimals to the values. Add a bottom border to the cell range **A16:B16**.

Accepted Density	Substance
11.35	Lead
7.87	Iron
10.49	Silver
2.70	Aluminum
8.90	Nickel
0	Invalid Result

b. Select Column B and change the column width to 12.75.

c. Select the range **A17:B22** and sort the table **Smallest to Largest**.

d. Assign a range name **Identity** to the lookup table.

e. Create a VLOOKUP function in **cell C14** that returns the name of the substance based on the average density. Use the range name you just created for the table array.

Create the X, Y (Scatter) Chart

A useful way to view and present the data is with a graph, which provides a visual summary of the experiment. You will need to show the linear relationship for the densities of each sample and add a trendline to show linear regression.

a. Select the values only, for the volume and mass of each sample (range **B4:C9**).

b. Click the INSERT tab, click **Insert Scatter** (X, Y) or Bubble Chart, and then choose **Scatter**.

c. Move the chart below the lookup table and resize to span the range **A24:I41**.

d. Select the Chart Title placeholder and type **Density of Aluminum**. Apply bold and 20 pt font to the title.

e. Add axis titles: **Volume (mL)** to the primary horizontal axis and **Mass (g)** to the primary vertical axis. Apply bold and 12 pt font to the labels.

f. Format the horizontal axis so that the minimum bound is 2.0 since all volumes start after this point.

g. Add a linear trendline and choose the options to Set Intercept and Display Equation on chart.

h. Save and close the workbook.

Create and Format a Table

Your biology experiment on yeast fermentation under a variety of conditions has been completed. You have created a worksheet for the all of the fermentation data and one for just the results of one the substances. You want to work with the data using Excel's table features but also may need to work with your original worksheet, so you decide to copy the worksheet first and convert the data to a table.

a. Open the *05e_FermentationLab* workbook and save it as **05e_FermentationLab_LastFirst**.

b. Select the **Fermentation Data** worksheet and copy it to a new worksheet. Rename the duplicate worksheet **Fermentation Data Table**. Change the tab color of the new sheet to **Blue**. Move the Fermentation Data Sheet table to the right of the Fermentation Data worksheet.

c. Click any cell within the data range **A4:P25** and convert the data to a table.

d. Apply the **Table Style Medium 6** table style.

e. Delete Column C in the table, since 0 minutes is not needed for the analysis.

f. Merge and center the title over the range **A1:P1**, change the font size to 16 pt, and then apply **Blue, Accent 5 fill color**.

Filter and Sort the Table Data, and Use a Structured Reference

As you look over your results, you would like to try to analyze it. You decide that you should sort the data alphabetically by the substance and the concentration of each substance. Filtering the results for the substances where you had significant amounts of fermentation will also aid you in deciding what were good substrates for yeast.

a. Create a custom sort on the Fermentation Data Table worksheet, where the first-level sort is by substance in A–Z order and a second level is by concentration in smallest to largest order.

b. Filter the data to display only the following substances: **Ethanol**, **NaCl**, and **Sucrose**.

c. Add a new field to the right of the 65 minute field. Rename the new field **Good for Fermentation**, apply Wrap Text to the cell, and then change the column width to 14.50.

d. Create a formula with a structured reference, using the IF function, that determines if the amount of CO_2 production at 65 minutes is greater than or equal to 2.0; if so, it will display the word *Yes*; otherwise it will display the word *No*.

Apply Conditional Formatting

To highlight the values at 15 minute intervals, you decide to apply conditional formatting to illustrate the differences.

a. Apply the **Orange Data Bar** conditional formatting in the *Gradient Fill* section to the 30 minute interval.

b. Apply the **Green Data Bar** conditional formatting in the *Gradient Fill* section to the 45 minute interval.

c. Apply the Highlight Cells Rules, Greater Than conditional formatting to the 60 minute interval, where values greater than 1.5 are formatted with **Light Red Fill with Dark Red Text**.

d. Create a new conditional format that applies bold red font where the values equal Yes in the *Good for Fermentation* column.

e. Select the *Good for Fermentation* column and center the data.

f. Select and center all of the column headings.

Create a Line Chart

The results for salt (NaCl) are interesting, in that you would not have expected salt to be a good choice for yeast fermentation. You know that salt is added to bread dough to stimulate the yeast's ability to raise the dough. At differing concentrations, it appears that it does make a difference in the amount of CO_2 created, as indicated by the rise in volume in the pipette. You have isolated the results for NaCl and decide to create a line chart to visualize the changes over time.

a. Select the range **A5:N9** on the NaCl worksheet. Create a line chart.

b. Move the chart to its own sheet named **Line Chart**.

c. Apply the chart Layout 4 from the Quick Layout gallery.

d. Insert the chart title: **NaCl Concentration Evaluation**.

e. Add axis titles: **Minutes** on the primary horizontal axis and **Volume (mL)** on the primary vertical axis.

f. Move the legend to the right.

Finalize the Workbook

You want to prepare the fermentation lab workbook in case someone wants to print any of the worksheets. To ensure the worksheets print only on one page, you need to adjust the page setup options.

a. Create a footer on each worksheet with your name, the sheet name code, and the file name code.

b. Apply landscape orientation to the **NaCl** worksheet. Change the scaling so that all the columns fit on one page and the gridlines will print.

c. Apply landscape orientation to the **Fermentation Data Table** worksheet. Change the scaling so the sheet fits on one page.

a. Save and close the workbook. Submit based on your instructor's directions.

Use Microsoft Access

Background

Databases are an important tool in assisting scientists as a way of storing and analyzing data collected from scientific experiments and published literature. Microsoft Access can be used to create and maintain tables, create and edit queries, and create forms and reports.

Tasks

Scientific research, whether it be from experiments performed or knowledge collected, may require a way of organizing, storing, and analyzing information. This information could include the following:

- Creating tables and forms
  - Literature data
  - Experimental data
  - Observational data
  - Reference data
- Sorting, filtering, and querying data
- Creating relationships between tables
- Creating reports

Skills

The need to store, manage, and analyze data requires that students should be able to do the following:

Chapter 1

- Add, edit, and delete records
- Compact the database
- Sort table data
- Create, modify, and remove filters
- Understand relational power

Chapter 2

- Create and modify a table
- Share data
- Establish table relationships
- Create a single-table query
- Specify query criteria for different data types
- Understand query sort order
- Run, copy, and modify a query
- Create a multi-table query
- Modify a multi-table query

Chapter 3

- Create calculated field in a query
- Format and save calculated results
- Use built-in functions in Access
- Add aggregate functions to datasheets
- Create queries with aggregate functions

Chapter 4

- Create forms using form tools
- Use form views
- Sort records in a form
- Create reports using report tools
- Use report views
- Modify a report
- Apply conditional formatting

SCIENCE PROFESSIONALS

Capstone Exercises

You have a work-study job as a laboratory assistant in the biology department. The professor has been assessing the health of the Grove Run Creek that flows into Lake Wellburk. Students have been collecting water and aquatic life samples from April through November to check chemical and biological indicators. The water samples have been analyzed by a local testing facility, and students have identified the aquatic organisms. A database has already been created to store the collected data on the water samples. You have been asked to review the data and set up the database so that more data can be easily entered and manipulated. You will create and edit tables, queries, forms, and reports. The data from the testing facility is in an Excel file, and you will import that data into your Access database.

Use the Existing Database

After reviewing the data that was collected and with input from the professor about what information will be expected for reports, you are ready to review the database currently in use.

a. Open the database as *05a_GroveCreek* and save it as **05_ GroveCreek_LastFirst**. Enable Content.

b. Open the *Samples* table and examine the data.

c. Sort the Samples table in ascending order by the SiteID field.

d. Click **SAVE** on the Quick Access toolbar to save the sort to the table.

e. Correction for record S00002. The StudentID is incorrect. Change the StudentID from 010225 to 034889.

f. Switch to Design view and change the field size for SampleID to 6 and the StudentID field size to 6.

g. Format the CollectionDate field to Short Date.

h. Save the table. Click **YES** in the warning dialog box to continue, as the existing data will not be lost due to formatting the Collection Date field. Close the table.

Create the Sites Table

You need to create a table to store the names and locations of the sites where the samples were collected.

a. Create a new table in Design View.

b. Create a **SiteID** field that will function as the primary key, data type of Short Text, field size of 3.

c. Add a second field named **SiteName** with data type as Short Text and a field size of 25.

d. Add a third field named **Location**. It will have a data type of Short Text and a field size of 50.

e. Save the table with the name **Sites** and switch to Datasheet view. Enter the records into the new table:

SiteID	SiteName	Location
C01	Bolton	Route 29 South Marker 10
C02	Upper Bolton	Route 118 West Marker 20
C03	Elm Woods	Elm Road Marker 30
C04	Smith Farm	Smith Farm Road Marker 40
C05	Overbrook	Daisy Lane Marker 50

f. Adjust the column widths to Best Fit.

g. Save and close the table.

Create the Researcher Table

You need to create a table to store the names of the students who collected the samples.

a. Create a new table in Design View.

b. Add field names and data types as listed below. Adjust the field properties accordingly:

Field Name	Data Type	Field Properties	
StudentID	Short Text	Field Size: 6	
FirstName	Short Text	Field Size: 20	Caption: First Name
LastName	Short Text	Field Size: 25	Caption: Last Name
Experience	Yes/No		

c. Set the StudentID field as the Primary Key.

d. Save the table with the name **Researcher**.

e. Switch to Datasheet view. Enter the records into the new table:

StudentID	First Name	Last Name	Experience
010225	Michael	Wilkes	Yes
023311	Diana	Shroyer	No
034562	Robert	Yerke	Yes
034889	James	King	No
040254	Addyson	Burkley	Yes
054321	Your First Name	Your Last Name	No

f. Close the table.

Share Data with Excel

The table that stores the sample results, Samples, is missing the data for July through November. The data was recorded in an Excel spreadsheet by the previous work-study student. You now need to bring the data into the Access database, adding the data to the existing Samples table.

a. Append the data of the **05a_CreekSampleResults** Excel file to the Samples table.

b. Open the *Samples* table and examine the data.

c. Verify the number of samples. There should be a total of 40 records.

d. Close the table.

Establish Table Relationships

Now that all of the tables have been designed and populated, it is time to create relationships between the tables so you can extract the data efficiently. You will set the relationships and enforce referential integrity.

a. Open the Relationships window. Add all of the tables to the Relationships window and close the Show Table window.

b. Create a relationship between the Researcher table and the Samples table by dragging the **StudentID** field in the Researcher table onto the StudentID field in the Samples table. Enforce referential integrity.

c. Create a relationship between the Sites table and the Samples table by dragging the SiteID field in the Sites table and the SiteID field in the Samples table. Enforce referential integrity.

d. Save and close the Relationships window.

Create a Form Using a Form Tool

You need to create a form to enter additional sample data that will be collected for Part 2 of the project.

a. Create a form based on the Samples table.

b. Change the title label to **Streams Entering Lake Wellburk Sample Results**.

c. Reduce the size of the text box controls to approximately 2" wide.

d. Select the labels, apply Bold formatting, and then change the font color to Dark Blue (under Standard Colors).

e. Switch to Form View and add the following new record:

SampleID	S00041
SiteID	C01
StudentID	054321
CollectionDate	11/30/2014
FC	2
EC	3
NITRATE	0.01
IRON	1
OXYGEN	10.8
PH	6.5

TURB	8
ALK	6
TP_P	0.03

f. Save the form as **Sample Testing Results** and close the form.

Create Filters

You need to quickly identify all of the samples collected after April 1, 2014, where the EC count is greater than 1. High EC counts are known to be an issue with drinking-water quality.

a. Open the Samples table in Datasheet view.

b. Use Filter by Form to filter the records to find all of the samples collected after 4/1/2014 with EC > 1.

c. Apply the filter. Copy the resulting records. Create a new blank table in datasheet view. Click on Paste, and choose Paste Append, to add them into a new table. Save the table as **HighEC**.

d. Add a Totals row to the HighEC table. Display the maximum FC and the minimum EC values.

e. Apply a Filter by Selection to the HighEC table where SiteID equals C04.

f. Save and close the HighEC table.

g. Close the Samples table and do not save the changes.

Create Single-Table Queries

You need to create a query to analyze all of the samples collected in July 2014 and a query to display all samples where the pH is less than 6.5.

a. Create a query in Design view; include all fields from the Samples table.

b. Add criteria to show all records where the collection date is between 7/1/2014 and 7/31/2014.

c. Run the query. Save the query as **July 2014 Samples**.

d. Verify that the results are only from July. Close the query.

e. Create a query in Design view; include the SampleID, SiteID, and PH fields from the Samples table.

f. Add criteria to show all records where the PH field is less than 6.5.

g. Run the query. Save the query as **Unacceptable PH Samples**.

h. Review the results and close the query.

Create a Multi-Table Query

You need to create a query to see if there is any correlation to some of the sample result differences due to inexperienced students collecting the samples.

a. Create a query in Design view. Add the Researcher, Samples, and Sites tables to the Design grid.

b. Add the SampleID field from the Samples table; the SiteName and Location from the Sites table; and the FirstName, LastName, and Experience fields from the Researcher table. Then, from the Samples table, add in the CollectionDate, FC, and PH fields.

c. Add criteria to display only those records from students with no experience.

d. Run the query and save the query as **Samples Collected by Inexperienced Students**.

Create a Calculated Field in a Query

The bacterial counts can be combined for analysis. You need to create a query that adds the FC and EC counts together for each sample.

a. Create a query in Design view using the Samples table; include the SampleID, SiteID, CollectionDate, FC, and EC fields.

b. Save the query as **Total Coliforms Count**.

c. In the first blank column in the query design grid, create a calculated field named TotalColiforms that adds the FC and EC fields together.

d. Format the property-sheet caption for the calculated field to Total Coliform Count.

e. Run the query. Check to see that the calculated field has correctly added the FC and EC fields. Adjust all fields to Best Fit.

f. Return to Design view and do not display the FC and EC fields. Save and close the query.

Use Functions in a Query

To make some of the data easier for review, you will create a calculated field to display "Acceptable" or "Unacceptable" for samples where the water meets drinking standards for iron content.

a. Create a query in Design view using the Samples table; include SampleID, SiteID, and CollectionDate fields from the Samples table.

b. In the first blank column in the query design grid, use the Expression Builder to create a field called **IronMCL**, using the IIf function. The string "Acceptable" will be applied if the iron value is <= .3, otherwise the string "Unacceptable" will be applied.

c. Run the query. Save the query as **Iron Maximum Contaminant Levels**.

d. Copy the Iron Maximum Contaminant Levels query and save it as **Unacceptable Iron Contaminant Levels**.

e. Run the query, if necessary. Apply a filter to view only those records which are unacceptable.

f. Save the filter and close the query.

Create a Totals Query

You need to analyze all of the sample testing data by site to arrive at the Average, Minimum, and Maximum counts for some of the tests performed.

a. Create a query in Design view using the Sites and Samples tables; include SiteName from the Sites table, and the OXYGEN, TURB, and TP_P fields from the Samples table.

b. Display the Total row. Calculate the average OXYGEN, minimum TURB, and maximum TP_P.

c. Change the field property for AvgofOXYGEN to Fixed.

d. Run the query. Save the query as **Oxygen, Turbidity, and Phosphorus Results by Site**.

e. Close the query.

Create a Report Using the Report Wizard

The professor has asked you to create a report representing the sample results by site so a decision can be made on further sample testing.

a. Use the Report Wizard to create a report. Choose SiteName from the Sites table. Choose all of the fields from the Samples table except SampleID, SiteID, and StudentID.

b. Accept the defaults for Grouping. Sort in ascending order by CollectionDate.

c. Add Summary options, showing Detail and Summary, and choose Avg for all fields listed.

d. Choose the Stepped Layout and the Landscape Orientation.

e. Save the Report as **Preliminary Sample Results**.

f. Change the Format property of the TP_P field to Fixed.

g. Modify the column width of the TP_P label and text box so that all data is visible.

h. Change the Format property of all of the Avg field text boxes to Fixed.

i. Modify any other labels and text boxes to keep the fields nicely spaced, and all data visible.

j. Delete the Summary for "SiteID" control in the SiteID footer.

k. Apply conditional formatting for the FC field to display values greater than 2, with the font color red (standard color).

l. View the report in Report view to make sure it will display on one page only. Save and close the report.

Compact, Repair, and Back Up the Database

To make sure that your database operates efficiently and securely, you are going to compact the database and create a duplicate copy of your database as a backup.

a. Compact and repair the database.

b. Back up the database in the location where you save your student files. Accept the default file name and save it.

c. Submit the database based on your instructor's directions.

Use Microsoft PowerPoint

Background

College students majoring in the sciences will often be required to present the results of their findings. Microsoft PowerPoint makes it possible to create presentations with media objects, charts and graphs, transitions, and animations to aid in delivering results to an audience. Being able to communicate one's work visually using Microsoft PowerPoint is a necessary skill.

Tasks

A formal lab report or scientific paper may often need to be presented to a group. Presentations and documents created using PowerPoint could include the following:

- Presentations for the results of experiments
- Presentations for educational purposes
- Informative presentations displayed at workshops
- Printed handouts

Skills

PowerPoint can be used to convey information visually, teach a concept, and more. Students should be able to do the following:

Chapter 1

- Use PowerPoint views
- Insert media objects
- Add a table
- Use animations and transitions
- Insert a header and footer
- Run and navigate a slideshow

Chapter 2

- Modify an outline structure
- Reuse slides from an existing presentation
- Use sections
- Modify a theme
- Modify a slide master

Chapter 3

- Create shapes
- Apply Quick Styles and customize shapes
- Create SmartArt
- Modify SmartArt
- Create WordArt
- Modify WordArt

Chapter 4

- Insert a picture
- Transform a picture
- Add audio
- Change audio settings

SCIENCE PROFESSIONALS

Capstone Exercises

It is important that science majors are knowledgeable in creating their laboratory and scientific reports. Since you have written several successful reports, your instructor has asked you to prepare a slide-show in PowerPoint and present it to several classes. Your slideshow will cover the key points of writing scientific reports and of data us-age. In addition, your instructor has asked that you include the usage of charts or graphs, images and audio.

Create a New Presentation

You create a title slide for the new presentation and insert clipart to make it more interesting.

a. Create a new blank PowerPoint presentation and save it as **05p_Guidelines_LastFirst**.

b. Enter the following text in the placeholders of the Title slide:

- Title placeholder: **Guide to Writing Scientific Laboratory Reports**

- In the Subtitle placeholder, type your name.

c. Create a handout header with your name and a handout footer with your instructor's name and your class. Include the page number and current date.

d. Apply the **Retrospect** theme.

e. Change the color of the theme to **Blue Warm**.

f. Insert an online picture from Office.com clip art and search for "microscope." Insert the first image (*Silhouette of microscope*) on the title slide.

g. Change the Scale Height to 30%.

h. Move the image to the top-right corner of the slide. Click the Size Dialog Box Launcher and Position to set the horizontal position 10" from the top-left corner and the vertical position 5" from the top-left corner.

i. Apply the Picture Effect, Soft Edges, 5 pt to the image.

Add Existing Content to the Presentation

You have previously created a simple slide show with no format-ting for this assignment and decide to use most of it for this pre-sentation. You will add these slides to your existing presentation first and then add a new slide to the end of the show.

a. Reuse slides 2 through 14 from *05p_Writing.pptx*.

b. View the slide show to familiarize yourself with the contents.

c. Insert a new slide at the end of the slide show, using the **Blank** layout.

d. Insert a WordArt image with **Fill - Black, Text 1, Outline – Back-ground 1, Hard Shadow – Background 1** and type **Any Questions?**

e. Format the WordArt, using the Text Effect **Glow, Blue, 18 pt. glow, Accent color 3**.

Insert a Table

To demonstrate what a data table should look like, you decide to include one in the presentation.

a. Change the layout of slide 14 (*Tables*) to the **Two Content** layout.

b. Insert a table with three columns and five rows into the place-holder on the right.

Sample	Volume (mL)	Mass (g)
1	6.0	17.20
2	7.0	17.76
3	6.2	17.08
4	7.2	18.06

c. Center the column titles and the column with the sample numbers.

d. Right align the values for the volume and mass of samples 1–4.

e. Select table and change the font size to **24 pt**.

f. Resize the table to a height of **4"** and a width of **5"**.

g. Apply the **Light Style 2** table style.

Create SmartArt and Add a Shape

You decide that the presentation would be more interesting if you used SmartArt features to define the importance of each section of the report, rather than using a bulleted list.

a. Select slide 4 and convert the bulleted list to SmartArt, choos-ing **Vertical Box List** as your SmartArt layout.

b. Change the color of the SmartArt image to **Colorful-Accent Colors**.

c. Apply the SmartArt style **Polished**.

d. Click on slide 10. Create a **Cloud Callout** shape.

e. In the callout type, **What is the specific purpose of this study?** Format the callout style to **Colored Fill-Blue, Accent 3**. Increase the font size to 20 pt.

f. Resize the callout to a height of **2.3"** and width of **2.3"**. Position the callout in the middle of your slide. Move the pointer part of the callout to point to the first sentence on the slide.

Inserting Images and Audio

Your slideshow needs a good ending to further enhance the pre-sentation. You decide to add a lab-related photo and an audio file to add interest also.

a. Click on slide 9 (*Introduction or Purpose*), and change the slide layout to **Two Content**.

b. Add an image to the right content placeholder by inserting the picture *05p_Scientist.jpg*.

c. Apply the Picture Effect **Shadow, Perspective Diagonal upper left** to the picture.

d. Go to the last slide in the slide show (*Any Questions?*) and insert an audio file, using the option Audio on My PC. Select the file *05p_Music.mid*. Set it to **Start Automatically** and **Hide During Show.**

e. Position the sound icon to the bottom-right corner of the slide.

Create Sections and Modify the Outline Structure

As you review your presentation, you realize you could benefit from organizing your slides into sections and modify the outline structure by moving the section to another area of your slide show.

a. Add a section named **Format** between slides 2 and 3.

b. Add a section named **Guidelines** between slides 6 and 7.

c. Add a section named **Structure** between slides 8 and 9.

d. Add a section named **Help** between slides 14 and 15.

e. Collapse all slides, move the **Guidelines** section above the **Format** section, and then expand all slides.

f. Switch to Outline View and go to slide 9. Increase the list level of the last four lines on slide, beginning with Equipment and ending with Methods used.

g. Return to Normal View.

Modify the Slide Master

While reviewing the presentation, you notice that the font size is too small on your bulleted lists. The quickest way to change the font on all of the slides is to edit the Slide Master.

a. View the Slide Master. Click the top slide in the left pane and make the following changes:

    1. Select the first level of text in the content placeholder (Click to edit Master text styles) and change the font size to **28 pt**.

    2. Edit the second level of text to **24 pt** font.

    3. Edit the third level of text to **22 pt** font.

    4. Edit the fourth level of text to **20 pt** font.

b. Save the changes and close Master View.

Finalize the Presentation

You are now ready to add animations to the presentation to add interest and apply a transition effect to the slides.

a. Select the bullet placeholders on slide 2, apply the **Underline** animation, and then set the animation to start After Previous.

b. Select the SmartArt on slide 6 and apply the **Float In** animation. Add the **One By One** effect option.

c. Apply the **Page Curl** transition to all slides.

d. View the presentation.

e. Save and close the **05p_Guidelines_LastFirst** and submit based on your instructor's directions.

Integrate Microsoft Office Programs

Background

When it comes using Microsoft Office, many Office programs can accomplish the same basic task, but knowing which one is best suited for a particular project is important. It is important to think about what the end result should look like, how complicated it will be to get there, and what features are needed to accomplish the goal. Microsoft Word is best utilized when creating lab and scientific reports. Microsoft Excel is utilized for graphing, charting, and calculating data. Microsoft Access is the best choice for managing large amounts of data that have been collected and when queries and reports need to be generated. Microsoft PowerPoint is valuable for creating presentations to report experimental findings and explain scientific principles. At times, several programs are used to create a final document or report, as needed to create the desired results.

Tasks

Students majoring in the sciences will need to know how to integrate data among the Office programs. This could include the following:

- Creating documents such lab reports, scientific papers, and correspondence
- Create worksheets to analyze data and visually interpret the data by creating charts
- Copy and paste data among applications
- Import data from Excel into Access
- Import data from an Access database
- Create queries

Skills

In addition to basic skills in each of the Office programs, students should be able to do the following:

- Create graphs and charts from Excel data
- Paste Excel worksheets or charts into a Word document
- Import data from Excel into Access
- Create queries with calculated fields
- Create a report in Access
- Format a document
- Use Mail Merge

Capstone Exercises

You are working as a lab assistant in the biology department at your school, where you, several other students, and the professor have been collaborating on a research project they are hoping to publish. The project consists of a survey that was developed and completed by student volunteers to assess weight gain and behavioral patterns during college that may contribute to overweight and obesity in later life.

The data was collected using Access, and the initial observations were obtained by applying filters to the results of the survey table. By exporting the survey results into Excel, it may be easier to use some of its features for the statistics. You need to create some queries in an Access database to analyze the rest of the data. The research report has been written but is not complete. You need make some changes to the report and create some graphs (charts). You have also been asked to send out a thank-you letter along with a gift card to the students who completed the survey and will create a mail merge to facilitate sending them.

Import Data from an Access Database

Measurements of student height and weight were obtained in the fall semester. At the end of the spring semester, all students were weighed again. The initial results from the fall semester were entered in a table in a different Access database. You need to import that table into the current database. You need to create a relationship between tables to ensure query results will be accurate.

a. Open *05i_Survey* database and save it as **05i_Survey_LastFirst**. Enable content.

b. Import external data from Access, using the *05i_SpringResults* database, choosing the **SpringWeighIn** table to import. Do not save the import steps.

c. Create a one-to-one relationship and enforce referential integrity between the **SpringWeighIn** table and the **SurveyResults** table.

d. Save the relationship and close the Relationship window.

Import Data from Excel into Access

The student government association has provided you with the names and addresses of the students who participated in the survey. You need to import them into the database to keep all of the data for the survey in one place and to be able to send the students a thank-you letter. You need to create a relationship between the tables in the database.

a. Import external data from Excel, using the *05i_SurveyAddresses* workbook, to import the source data into a new table in the current database. Indicate that the first row contains column headings, with StudentID as the primary key, and accept Addresses as the table name. Do not save the import steps.

b. Create a one-to-one relationship and enforce referential integrity between the **Addresses** table and the **SurveyResults** table.

c. Save the relationship and close the Relationship window.

Create Queries with Calculated Fields

The only query that has been done determines the body mass index (BMI) at the beginning of the fall semester. Now, you need to create additional queries about BMI and weight gain.

a. Create a query to determine the BMI for the end of the spring semester. Include the StudentID and Weight2 fields from the SpringWeighIn table and the Height field from the SurveyResults table. Create a calculated field for the body mass index; type **FinalBMI: Weight2*703/(Height*Height)**.

b. Format the field to Fixed and display only two decimals. Do not display the Height field. Save the query as **FinalBMI**.

c. Create a query to determine the amount of weight gain per student. Include the StudentID and Weight1 fields from the SurveyResults table and the Weight2 field from the SpringWeighIn table. Create a calculated field named **WeightGain** that calculates the difference between the Weight2 and Weight1 fields.

d. Run the query. Add a Total row to the datasheet and determine the average weight gain. Save the query as **WeightGainPerStudent**.

e. Copy the WeightGainPerStudent query and save it as **EatingHabits**.

f. Add the following fields from the SurveyResults table: Q01, Q02, Q03, Q04, Q05, Q06, and Q07. Do not display the Weight1 and Weight2 fields.

g. Run the query. Use Filter by Selection to display records where WeightGain is not equal to 0. Change the Total row for the WeightGain field to Count. Save and close the query.

Create a Report

The advisor for the research project has asked you to create a report in Access to display the eating habits of the students who gained weight, especially how many times a day they consume snack foods, exercise, and spend time watching TV or using the computer.

a. Use the Report Wizard to create the report, choosing the WeightGain field from the WeightGainPerStudent query and the Q05, Q08, and Q12 fields from the SurveyResults table.

b. Accept all of the default settings except for the layout. Choose Landscape layout and save the report as **Weight Gain Analysis**.

c. Modify the report so that the labels and text boxes are nicely spaced and all data and labels are visible.

d. Apply conditional formatting for the WeightGain field to display values greater than 5, with the font color Red (standard color). Save and close the report.

Import Data in Excel and Create a Chart

A worksheet with statistics needs to be created, and you decide to export the data from Access into Excel. You need to create another query first and will then export the query to Excel and use the data to create a chart. Additional data to create another chart needs to be entered into Excel.

a. Create a query using the Query Wizard. Select the **Gender field** from the SurveyResults table, the BMI field from the IntialBMI query, and the FinalBMI field from the FinalBMI query.

b. Select **Summary** and choose **Summary Options**, selecting Avg for both BMI fields. Save the query as **BMIComparision** and select the option to modify the query.

c. Change the caption for the Avg of BMI field to Avg Initial BMI and change the caption for the Avg of FinalBMI field to Avg Final BMI. Run the query and adjust the column widths so the field names are visible.

d. Export the BMIComparison query into Excel. Save the workbook to the same location as the Access database and name it **05i_SurveyStatistics_LastFirst.xlsx**.

e. Export the data with formatting and layout and open the destination file after the export operation is complete. Do not save the export steps. Close Access.

f. Select **cells A1:C3** of the BMIComparison worksheet and create a clustered column chart. The chart title should be **All Students by Gender**. Move the chart directly under the data.

g. Insert a new worksheet and name it **Exercise**. Enter the text and data listed below into the worksheet starting at **cell A3**. Widen columns as necessary.

Exercise Type	Female	Male
Aerobic Exercise (3 or more times/week)	11	8
Stretching (2–3 times/week)	5	9
Strength training (2–3 times/week)	2	12
At least one of the above	26	18
No exercise	20	20

h. Select **cells A3:C8** and create a clustered column chart. The chart title should be **Exercise Type by Gender**. Move the chart directly under the data.

i. Save the workbook. Do not close the workbook.

Format the Document and Insert the Charts

The research report is still a work in progress. You need to insert a watermark so it is not accidentally released before it is reviewed by everyone. It is also missing page numbers, and the footnotes need to be converted to endnotes. You also need to insert the charts you created in Excel into the report before you pass it along for further review and completion.

a. Open the *05i_WeightChange* document and save it as **05i_WeightChange_LastFirst**.

b. Insert a custom diagonal watermark, with the text **For Review Only**, and change the font color to Red.

c. Insert a page number at the bottom of page, using the Bold Numbers 2 style.

d. Click the **References tab** and open the Footnotes dialog box in the Footnotes group. Convert the footnotes to endnotes.

e. Insert the **All Students by Gender** chart from the BMIComparison worksheet to page 4 under the heading *GRAPH 1: BMI Comparison*, using Paste Special to paste it as a Microsoft Excel Chart Object.

f. Insert the **Exercise Type by Gender** chart from the Exercise worksheet under the heading *GRAPH 2: Exercise Comparison* (bottom of page 4), using Paste Special to paste it as a Microsoft Excel Chart Object.

g. Save and close the document.

h. Save and close the workbook.

Create a Mail Merge to Send Out Letters

You created a thank-you letter to send to the survey participants and are now ready to make the final formatting changes and complete a mail merge. You will save the mail-merged letters for printing on school letterhead and mailing next week when the gift cards are sent over from the student government coordinator.

a. Open the *05i_ThankYou* document and save it as **05i_Thankyou_LastFirst**.

b. Start mail merge by using the Step-by-Step Mail Merge Wizard to select the Letters mail merge process.

c. Use the current document to start the letter.

d. Select recipients, using an existing list, from the Addresses table in the *05i_Survey_LastFirst* database. Refine the recipient list by sorting it by LastName in ascending order.

e. Insert an address block using the default form of *Joshua Randall Jr.* as the recipient name and accept the other defaults.

f. Press Enter twice and insert a greeting line in the form of *Dear Joshua:*

g. Preview your letters to verify the address block and greeting lines are correct.

h. Complete the merge step but do not print any of the documents (you would have 100 letters). Save the merged letter file as **05i_Merged_LastFirst** and close the document.

i. Save 05i_ThankYou_LastFirst letter and close the document.

j. Submit the files as directed by your instructor.

Index